CELTIC
Wisdom
Sticks

CELTIC Wisdom Sticks

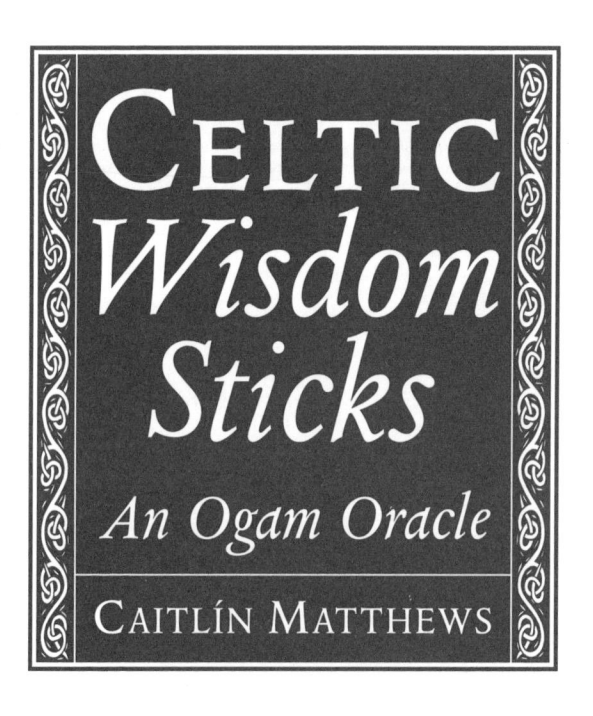

An Ogam Oracle

CAITLÍN MATTHEWS

CONNECTIONS
BOOK PUBLISHING

For Jane Gubb who knows the woods and their kennings by hand and heart.

AUTHOR'S NOTE

In order to go to the roots of ogam, I have worked directly from the poetic kennings of the source texts: *Auraicept n'Eces* or the Scholar's Primer, as well as drawing upon works like the *Leabhar Bhaile an Mhóta* or Book of Ballymote, and an array of modern scholarship. The ogam oracle of the Celtic Wisdom Sticks has been conceived through a fusion of textual research, poetic insight and shamanic analepsis or far-remembering by which the Irish *filid* (poets) used to discover lost or forgotten information. I fully expect that the user will also access other levels of this sophisticated memory system by means of tactile contact with the ogam sticks themselves.

Irish names and titles appear with a rough pronunciation in brackets: exact speech equivalents can only be approximate. The stress should be placed on the syllable before the apostrophe, for example Emancoll (E'man-col.). Languages do not stand still, however, and Irish is no exception. I have chosen to use the middle Irish spelling and pronunciation of *ogam* (O'gum). In modern Irish, however, it is written *ogham* and pronounced O'am.

Caitlín Matthews,
Oxford, 8 January 2001

NOTE: *there may be natural variations in the sticks, which are made of real wood.*

A CONNECTIONS EDITION
First published in Great Britain in 2001 by Connections Book Publishing Limited
St Chad's House, 148 King's Cross Road, London WC1X 9DH

This edition published in the U.S.A. in 2001 by Connections Book Publishing Limited
Distributed in the U.S.A. by Red Wheel/Weiser, P.O. Box 612, York Beach, ME 03910-0612

Text copyright © Caitlín Matthews 2001
Illustration copyright © Vanessa Card 2001
This edition copyright © Eddison Sadd Editions 2001

The right of Caitlín Matthews to be identified as the author of the work has been asserted by her in accordance with the Copyright, Designs and Patents Act 1988.

All rights reserved. No part of this book may be reproduced, stored in a retrieval system, or transmitted in any form or by any means without the prior written permission of the publisher, nor be otherwise circulated in any form of binding or cover other than that in which it is published and without a similar condition being imposed on the subsequent purchaser.

British Library Cataloguing-in-Publication data available on request.

ISBN 1-85906-053-6

10 9 8 7 6 5 4 3 2

Phototypeset in Columbus using QuarkXPress on Apple Macintosh
Produced by Hung Hing Offset Printing Co. Ltd.
Manufactured in China

Contents

Introduction 6

PART ONE
**Keys of Knowledge:
Origins of Ogam** 7

PART TWO
**Casting the Woods:
Divinatory Methods** 20

PART THREE
**Memory of the Trees:
Oracles and Meaning** 40

PART FOUR
**Fionn's Window:
Using your Intuition** 82

Further Reading 95

Acknowledgements 96

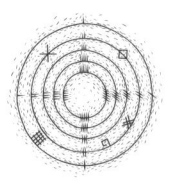

Introduction

You hold in your hands a potent set of keys that can open doors to spark memory and inspiration within you. The sticks are inscribed in ogam, the ancient Irish alphabetic script. Etched upon boundary and memorial stones around the seaboard of Ireland, Wales and Scotland, ogam dates from about the fourth century CE. Part One of this book gives a short background to ogam, its origin and ancient uses. Part Two shows how to use the ogam sticks for divination, with sample readings.

With the pouch accompanying this book there are twenty sticks with their bark stripped on two sides and their ogam title inscribed against the bare edge. The top of each of the sticks is blackened so that you can easily distinguish which way up the ogam symbol is to be read. The extra indicator stick has its bark stripped on all four sides and the cardinal directions inscribed around it to help determine the appropriate oracle for each ogam letter. You can keep your sticks in the pouch provided. The ogam oracles derive from the mysterious word hoards of the prophetic poets of ancient Ireland, and provide a series of eighty possible answers, which can be looked up in Part Three. A more intuitive and personal way of creating your own unique oracle, which invites you to share in the revelation that lies at the roots of the ogam mystery, is described in Part Four.

PART ONE

Keys of Knowledge: Origins of Ogam

Ogham is an alphabet of carved grooves. Vertical, horizontal, diagonal, single or grouped. Notation for music; a visual code for sounds. These sounds become names and stories and folklore. Prehistory is the world before words. Ogham breaks that spell. Ogham is the first sound-byte.

THE ALPHABET STONE DEREK HYATT

We do not know who invented ogam. The ancient sources available to us offer three mythic origins: a biblical one involving Fenius Farsaidh, a Scythian sage and incumbent of Nimrod's Tower, who was also a forerunner of the Gaelic people; a native Irish myth involving the Tuatha de Danaan god Ogma, the father of speech and poetry; and a bardic origin involving the great Milesian poet, Amairgin, the legendary originator of much poetic traditional lore.

The main text from which the ogam material is derived is the *Auraicept na n'Eces* or The Scholar's Primer, an introduction to the word-play of poetry through the grammar of the ogam alphabet. Its probable author is the historical seventh century poet,

Cenn Faelad. The *Auraicept* remains one of the liveliest expositions of oral tradition in transcribed form and also one of the most obscure. Scholars have attempted to discover various linguistic origins for the ogam alphabet, but it seems to have been a home-grown Irish alphabet, rooted in the oral, poetic tradition, giving access to the door of ancient memory.

Interest in ogam has been fuelled more recently by Robert Graves' book, *The White Goddess*. He identifies the ogam alphabet as a calendar, with each tree as a month. However, for the Irish, ogam was an alphabet, not a calendar. Theories of ogam as a cypher have been popular, the most pleasant being that of the late musicologist, Sean O'Boyle, who suggested that it might even have been a form of harp notation.

Knife and Branch

Whatever its origins, ogam was not merely a means of inscription. It was a tool of the guardians of the oral Gaelic wisdom, the *filid* (fil'ee) or oracular poets, whose task was to remember complex ancestral and traditional lore. For them the ogam letters were as sprigs from the great Tree of Wisdom which interpenetrates the earth with its roots, and the sky with its branches. For them each letter simultaneously represented the wisdom of its tree and the living language of an oral, poetic tradition which saw image, metaphor and association as the secret prophetic way to communicate meaning.

The key to ogam has so far rested on the misleading understanding that each of the titles of the individual letters represents a tree and only a tree. However, when we examine the alphabetical titles, we find that only five ogam letters are actually also names of trees: beith (birch), fearn (alder), saille (willow), duir (oak) and coll (hazel). The other fifteen letter names have other face meanings in Irish: for instance, gort means 'field', uir means 'earth' and straif means 'sulphur'. This is not widely understood by non-Gaelic speakers and has often been ignored in popular ogam literature.

Trees are only one set of criteria by which the alphabetical names have been remembered, although they have become the standard way of memorizing them. Many written scripts in world language derive originally from pictograms and have become formalized into script, but ogam has survived uniquely as a memory system of visualized associative values and images. The *Auraicept na n'Eces* says 'the names of the ogam letters were given *metaphorically* from the trees of the forest'. The fact that the Irish word for 'letter' is *fid* or *feda*, which means 'tree' or 'trees' also contributes to the alphabet's association with tree names. Ogam letters had many alternative associations – we find Bird-ogam, Work-ogam, Place-ogam, for example, each letter name being also a bird, occupation or place – but, for the sake of convenience, the letters were anciently represented by trees by which the alphabet

KEYS OF KNOWLEDGE

could be remembered as groves of living letters. As we study the ogam texts, it becomes clear that Tree Ogam is only one among many possible ogam alphabet names. In this book we cannot enter fully into such complex sets of associations that may anciently have formed a theatre of memory, whereby poets could communicate with each other in ogam. This book deals with Tree Ogam, although the oracles given in Part Three derive from a wider series of ogam 'kennings' or under-meanings, which would once have formed part of the poet's memory network of metaphor.

The Ogam Alphabet

The table to the right shows the twenty English letters, the ogam titles, tree correspondences and characters as they appear in the *Auraicept na n'Eces*, the chief source of ogam and upon whose wisdom this oracle is based. The ogam letters are given as the modern reader would read them, from top to bottom; however, when they are used in inscriptions ogams are read from the bottom up.

The twenty letters are further divided into their *aicmi* or tribes: the B-tribe (B, L, F, S, N) all have their strokes to the right of the *druim* or stemline, the H-tribe (H, D, T, C, Q) to the left, the M-tribe strokes (M, G, NG, STR, R) are diagonal to the stem, and the A-tribe strokes (A, O, U, E, I) pass left to right across the stem.

ORIGINS OF OGAM

LETTER	TITLE	TREE	OGAM	PAGE
B	Beith	Birch		42
L	Luis	Rowan		44
F	Fearn	Alder		46
S	Saille	Willow		48
N	Nin	Ash		50
H	Huath	Hawthorn		52
D	Duir	Oak		54
T	Tinne	Holly		56
C	Coll	Hazel		58
Q	Quert	Apple		60
M	Muin	Vine		62
G	Gort	Ivy		64
NG	NGetal	Fern		66
STR	STRaif	Blackthorn		68
R	Ruis	Elder		70
A	Ailm	Pine		72
O	Onn	Gorse		74
U	Uir	Heather		76
E	Edad	Aspen		78
I	Idad	Yew		80

KEYS OF KNOWLEDGE

Use of Ogam

It is evident that this alphabet is intended to be inscribed with a knife or chisel upon the edge of stone or wood rather than written in ink upon paper, since it uses a ridge or edge and straight strokes.

Images from Irish poetic lore support the idea of tree and knife. One of the most profound forms of poetic prophecy was called *teinm laegda*, literally 'stripping the pith or bark', whereby poets solved problems by peeling back poetic layers of meaning in an incantatory trance to discover the answer. The same image is used in the story of the mariner, Maelduin, where we are assured that Christ, like a master-poet in search of prophetic resolution to such mysteries, 'has successively stripped the bark of revelation'.

The texts tell us that 'the father of ogam is Ogma, the mother of ogam is the hand or knife of Ogma'. Ogma is the Irish god of poetry and eloquence: a member of the mythical Tuatha de Danaan tribe and a champion of his people.

Writing was not used by the Gaels and Britons – history, law, genealogy, stories, poetry and other branches of learning were maintained in memory and oral tradition. We know that druids and poets were familiar with other languages and could indeed both write and read them; but within their own language and culture, they maintained the sacred tradition of oral memory as the means of keeping learning fresh and alive. Such oral learning is more flexible than the written word,

ORIGINS OF OGAM

but the tradition can be lost unless it is safely passed on. In Ireland, the orally-learned classes soon gave way to clerics, for writing lent power under Christianity, just as oral memory once gave its exponents authority. By the eighteenth century poets were the only remaining exponents of an unbroken oral tradition.

Five extra letters, the *forfedha* (for'faya), were later added to the ogam alphabet. We can guess when they were added because it is known that the Latin alphabet contained only twenty letters in the fifth century, but by the seventh century it had acquired three extra letters to accommodate the 'barbarian' tongues of a wider Europe. There is a reference to the Breton St Samson of Dol being tutored by the British St Illtud in the early sixth century, learning his letters and their numerical equivalents from twenty letter squares and dice. Apart from representing the diphthongs, these extra letters were also used to denote the imported consonants not found in the Gaelic alphabet:

LETTER	TITLE	TREE	OGAM CHARACTER
EA	Ebhadh	Aspen	
OI	Oir	Spindle	
UI + Y	Uilleand	Honeysuckle	
IO + P	Iphin	Gooseberry	
AE + X	Phagos	Beech	

KEYS OF KNOWLEDGE

The Dark Language

The first everyday use of ogam seems to have been monumental, used to write personal names upon gravestones and boundary markers. But ogam is also found on ordinary personal objects such as brooches, knife-handles and weaving swords, as a mark of ownership. Simple name inscriptions on such objects and on public monuments like boundary stones were inscribed clearly in *ceart-ogam* or regular ogam that all might read them. But the ability to recognize each ogam letter did not, of itself, make for comprehension, since each letter also had its kennings or under-meanings which we will be drawing upon in Part Three.

Ogam seems to have been used as an encoded language in the hands of poets who were already accustomed to speaking the *dordacht,* or the 'dark language', to each other, obscuring what they were saying from the uninitiated. Poets maintained their status by virtue of their verbal dexterity, their formidable memory and their ability to divine the meanings of the unseen world. Masters of the spoken word, their sharp ears could catch both the surface and the under-meanings of poems and messages written or signed in ogam.

In Irish, as in many languages, a spoken word can have many meanings to the hearer. Irish poets played with these alternative meanings endlessly, being able to compose and recite a poem that had both an obvious meaning and an under-meaning. Here is an example of how words with several meanings were used. It is taken from *Coir Anmann* or 'The Aptness of Names', a poetic thesaurus of names and their meanings, and describes a woman named Fedelm who is called *Noíchruthach*: '... she was "nine-shaped" because nine appearances would come to her whenever she was beheld, or she was *Nua-chrothach*, "new-formed" because those who beheld her for the first time saw her beauty newly-minted, or she was *Nua-chraidech* "fresh-hearted" because of her great friendliness'. Each of the adjectives ascribed to Fedelm can be pronounced in Irish in so similar a way that the hearer is dependent upon the context for guidance as to the meaning.

Signing Ogam

We can imagine how short encoded ogam messages full of oracular and poetic import could be swiftly inscribed with a knife as sharp as the poet's tongue: messages that would have meaning for another poet, but which would confound the ignorant. Poets were not restricted to inscribing ogam: they might also sign in it. The fivefold divisions of ogam make it eminently suitable for signing with the hand. Indeed, it could have been communicated silently by gesture as modern signing is used by the deaf today. Texts cite Foot, Nose or Palm Ogam, which are thought to have been performed by placing the fingers of the hands across, respectively, the shinbone, the nose or the palm of the hand to indicate the shape and number of the strokes. However, there are no recorded instances of its use in this way in any story. There are plenty of references to inscribed stones and sticks.

It might be asked why any poet whose memory was phenomenal would wish to inscribe ogams on wood? In a training lasting twelve years during which poets were expected to learn the equivalent of a small library of stories, grammatical lore, prosody and historical precedent, everyone was aware that forgetfulness is ever the enemy of oral knowledge. In the *Baile in Scail*, or the 'Frenzy of the Apparition', when the god Lugh prophesies the future line of succession of the kings of Tara, we hear that 'Cesarn the poet found it difficult to memorize the incantation all at once and so he inscribed it in ogam upon four rods of yew. Each of these rods was twenty-four feet long and had eight sides'. Clearly Cesarn did not carry such unwieldy lengths of yew with him, but for such an important set of prophecies, it would have been wise to allow for the forgetfulness of future generations. This way, the prophecy would be remembered long after Cesarn was dead. Many ogam grave markers and boundary stones were clearly set up with this thought in mind.

Apart from inscribed marker stones, the most common usage of ogam was as a message or warning. Indeed, the very first use of ogam was as a warning sent to Lugh, son of Ethliu, saying, 'your wife will be abducted into the otherworld unless she is guarded by birch'. This message was etched upon a single birch twig with seven 'B's inscribed upon it. It was clearly not a verbally encoded message, where letters are substituted for other meanings, but something more obscure, possibly to do with number or frequency. We are told that this first use of the letter, and the wood on which it was written, gave birch or *beith* its precedence as the first letter of the alphabet. Sometimes warnings were encoded by the kennings, the short descriptive phrases that metaphorically represent each letter and which were learnt by poets.

Magic and Divination

Ogam was magical, each letter having its own special lore and power. We see its protective powers used in spells by the Ulster hero, Cuchullain, who attempts to slow down Medb's army by placing various complex ogam challenges in the way of the advance. The druids of the opposing army are forced not only to translate the challenge but to equal Cuchullain's dextrous achievements in creating their own. In one of these, the hero leaves a fallen oak tree inscribed with a secret ogam commanding that no-one may pass until a warrior is able to jump across the tree in his chariot.

Sometimes ogams are destructively written, as when young Corc is sent to Scotland with secret ogam markings written upon his shield, little knowing that they are an instruction to put its bearer to death.

Fortunately, a passing poet kindly alters the letters to bear a more favourable message while Corc sleeps.

But was ogam ever used for divination? Where writing, language and meaning meet is a magical threshold where meaning shimmers illusively. Although of a different origin, we may compare the runes of North western Europe with ogam. Runes can both represent spoken letters and be powerful symbols for fateful guidance. Examining the early Irish texts, we discover that ogam also has more than just its surface meanings. In *Tochmarc Etaine*, the druid Dallán is set to search for the missing Queen Etain by Eochaid, King of Tara. Dallán 'makes four yew rods, writing in ogam upon them until, through the keys of wisdom and his ogam craft, it is revealed to him that Etain has been born away by Midir to the faery hill of Brí Léith'. We are not told how he did this, but the text refers to the ogam letters as 'the keys of wisdom', indicating that ogam letters are keys to the door of the oral memory that evokes image and answer in a more than cryptological way.

The ability to read each ogam letter did not, of itself, make for comprehension, since each letter had its kennings, or under-meanings, which we will be drawing upon in Part Three. There is an Irish legend of a farmer who dreamed of a treasure buried under an oak tree. Under the treasure lay a stone on which were inscribed ogam markings. A poor travelling scholar asked if he could interpret the marks and read out, 'If this side is good, the other side is even better'. On digging deeper, an even greater store of treasure was found. This story exemplifies the very essence of ogam's mystery: the surface meaning is one thing, but what lies beneath is far, far richer. This ogam oracle uncovers that wealth of meaning, allowing the deep oracles of the under-meanings or kennings to directly answer the diviner when a question is posed.

In this short book it is impossible to say everything about ogam, or to consider every theory. Ogam remains mysteriously illusive as well as allusive. Rather than pile up examples of its use, we can take a leaf out of the *filid's* imagination and go playfully to the heart of the matter. In colloquial English, we sometimes say we 'twig' or understand a thing, little realizing that this expression derives from the Irish verb *tuigim*, meaning to understand or realize something. Each twig or ogam stick represents a storehouse of memory; each letter is a key that can open the door to knowledge and understanding for you. Now discover how you can use its wisdom.

PART TWO

Casting the Woods: Divinatory Methods

*If you're an asker, you'll be a knower,
poetry's knotty and wily –
the riddles you hear are windows,
and the door is enquiry.*

THE CHRISTIAN DRUIDS JOHN MINAHANE

When we consult an oracle, we come directly in touch with sources of wisdom beyond our own. To divine means 'to ask the gods'. Divination is not a tool for the curious. The integrity of the diviner plays an important part in all forms of divination. If we are in a respectful and attentive state when we consult the oracle, then we are in the best condition to understand its answers. You will find silence your best friend when it comes to seeking the heart of the oracle. Relax your body, still your mind's busy-ness, bring emotions to a place of calmness, so that you can elevate your spirit and bring it to a point of focus and attention. The diviner's wisdom derives from his or her ability to allow the oracle to speak for itself. The answer will be clearer if we don't attempt to impose our own fears, anxieties or self-pretensions upon the oracle.

Questioning the Oracle

Questions form the basis of much traditional Celtic oral teaching. A perfectly-worded question that springs from your need creates a pathway down which the oracle's answer can come to you. Framing and asking a question makes us feel vulnerable because it exposes our need. But once that need is stated, we cannot rest until the answer is received. Here are a few guidelines to help you frame your question:

1. *Do you actually want to ask this question? Whatever you ask is what you will be told about. Remember that when the answer has been given, you will have the responsibility for it: something you may not desire.*
2. *Is your question phrased to provide a suitable answer? Check each word to ensure that you mean what you say. Say the question aloud to check its authenticity.*
3. *Is your question conditional upon something? Avoid questions beginning 'should' or 'could'. Use formats like 'please show me the consequences of …' or 'I am concerned about … , please give me guidance about it.'*
4. *Is your question framed in a negative way? For example, 'Why don't I get better?' might be rephrased as 'What is the best pathway to health for me?'*
5. *Is there a need which takes precedence over the question you've chosen? You might trip-wire the question you didn't ask if you're unconsciously brooding upon something deeply seated but unstated.*
6. *Is your question framed only to give a yes/no answer? If*

so, rephrase it. However, if you want a yes/no answer, use the indicator stick. Roll it between your palms while considering your question. If South is facing you, then the answer is yes; if North, the answer is no. East or West means the matter is not yet concluded.

7. Does your question contain the phrase either/or? For example, 'Will Eric or Tom be a better partner for me?' Questions about choice are best handled during separate sessions or they confuse the oracle's answer.
8. Does your question feel lacking in energy? It should make your whole being sit up and sing. If there is no urgency or the wording is wrong, the question will fall flat and receive an offhand answer.
9. Does your question involve another person? Frame your question so that your own needs and issues are emphasized if your question is a legitimate one about an association or partnership.
10. Have you restricted your question or put conditions upon it? For example, the last part of the question 'How can I improve my work situation while living in a big city?' circumscribes it and dictates conditions to the oracle. Part of the answer may be that the querent (questioner) needs to move elsewhere, for example!
11. Are you expecting a predictive answer? The oracle will tell you only about the conditions of your issue as you present them now. Rather than asking, 'When will I succeed as an artist?', a question like, 'What factors will hasten my success as an artist?' may be more helpful. See 'Divination and Time' on page 37.

DIVINATORY METHODS

Using the Ogam Sticks

The twenty sticks are inscribed with the tree name, letter and ogam marking of the ogam alphabet. Each of the ogam sticks has a possible four oracles attached to it. Once you have selected the stick or sticks to make a reading using one of the methods outlined in this part (or one of your own methods when you become more experienced in using the oracle) you need to find out which oracle attached to the stick answers your question. To do this you need to roll the indicator stick between your palms with your eyes closed. Stop rolling and open your eyes: the surface of the indicator stick facing you will indicate which compass direction designates your answer. These oracles are given in Part Three, offering simple guidance about a matter that can be taken at a surface level, but the metaphorical images of the oracle may open up much more detail if you engage with them in greater depth.

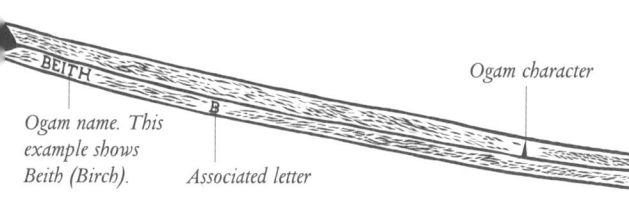

Ogam name. This example shows Beith (Birch).

Associated letter

Ogam character

Using the Indicator Stick

The indicator stick represents the great tree of otherworldly tradition that interpenetrates the starry heavens and the deep earth. As you roll it between

CASTING THE WOODS

your hands like someone making fire, you invoke the divine spark of creative inspiration into your divination question. The indicator stick is inscribed with four of the five *forfedha* or extra letters which represent the diphthongs. Although these form no part of the divinatory messages of this book, the four cardinal directions are associated with the winds that blow the branches of the tree and make music through their leaves. This is the reason that the extra letters of the ogam are inscribed upon the indicator stick – the message of the oracle changes as the winds change direction, just as the breath of a vowel or diphthong animates and changes the meanings of consonants. The direction in which the sacred winds of the universe are blowing determines everything in our everyday lives.

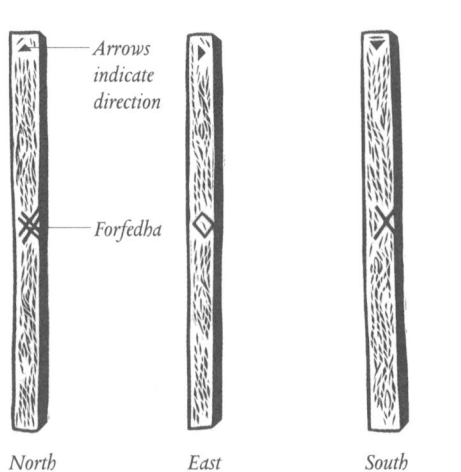

Arrows indicate direction

Forfedha

North   *East*   *South*   *West*

DIVINATORY METHODS

Reading for Others

You may wish to share the wisdom and memory of the trees with others and divine for friends or family. Take note of the following guidelines which will help maintain both your integrity as a diviner and your respect for the oracle:

1. *Respect other people's privacy – do not divine for those who haven't asked you to do so.*
2. *Divine appropriately: cast the ogam sticks at times and in places where they can be understood clearly and consulted sincerely, rather than frivolously or for the entertainment of the curious.*
3. *Avoid divining if you or your querent (the person with the question for whom you are divining) is in a very confused, medicated or inebriated condition, or when in a volatile state of mind.*
4. *Allow the oracle to unlock the answer without putting yourself or your concerns and opinions in the way of the door which is opening. (See 'Interpreting the Oracle' on page 36.)*
5. *Encourage the querent to ask a worthy, well thought-out question. Help them get to the root of the issue, if necessary by asking them clarifying questions.*
6. *Advise credulous or superstitious querents to take responsibility for their own life and be prepared to make changes. The ogam oracle gives us a true window into the state of the soul, but it does not dictate unchangeable or fated events.*

CASTING THE WOODS

Making a Simple Reading

Formulate your question carefully. Select an ogam stick for divination by one of the following methods: hold them all in one hand and with the other hand select one, or allow one to fall to the ground or on to a table. Alternatively, draw one unseen from the storage pouch. Whether you draw one twig or several (depending on the method you use) to help determine your question, each twig has a variety of answers.

When you have selected the stick or sticks for your reading, find the appropriate answer for each twig by rolling the four-sided indicator stick (*see page 24*). This has one of the cardinal directions inscribed upon each side. Roll it between your hands with your eyes closed. The side facing you when you stop will determine the appropriate answer for each twig, which can then be looked up in Part Three (*see table on page 11*). Here you will find a one-line answer for each letter, as well as a fuller oracular commentary, showing what wisdom is available to you from the twig, which has fallen from the otherworldly tree of knowledge into your hands. The following example of a one-stick reading shows just how far-reaching and meaningful even the most simple oracle can be:

DIVINATORY METHODS

SAMPLE READING: Marjory asked a question about changing jobs soon and selected the twig Luis (Rowan) with her eyes closed. She rolled the indicator stick between her hands; on stopping she found that the side facing her was West. Looking in Part Three under the entry for Luis, she read down the possible answers. Her oracle was under Luis – West:

'*You need to unknot the coil you have made. Retrace your steps and make amends.*' It further told her, '*When there is a muddle, it is impossible to continue without sorting things out – the coils can circumscribe further action or create further confusion. As with a tangled length of twine, start at one end and trace back patiently to the other end, stopping to untie any knots and snarls. When things are straightened, there can be movement again.*'

Marjory had to search her own motivations for wanting to change her job. A misunderstanding between her and her supervisor lay at the root of the problem; by leaving she could avoid further unpleasantness. The more difficult course of clearing matters up was not very attractive to her, but the oracle's question to her, 'What needs to be sorted out?' evoked a solution. In seeking another job, she would need a reference from her supervisor, and since this was Marjory's first job, it was not so easily set aside. After a few days of steeling herself, she requested an interview with the supervisor to try to clear matters up. The trouble had been due to an unclear instruction carelessly conveyed by one of Marjory's work-colleagues.

CASTING THE WOODS

With this explained to her supervisor, harmony was restored. Marjory felt happier about the situation and decided to give her job another chance.

Fionn's Ladder Reading

This four-twig reading is useful for gaining insight into the progress of things you have undertaken, or to give you a clearer overview of an issue. It is based on a quotation from the *Auraicept na n'Eces*, which gives us a valuable insight into the nature of the ogams.

> *'The B tribe lie to the right of the ridge; the H tribe lie to the left of the ridge; the M tribe lie across the ridge; the A tribe lie through the ridge ... This is how a tree is climbed: by treading upon the root of the tree first with the right hand and then with the left hand. Then across the trunk and around it.'*

The ogam letters are arranged up the *druim* or stemline in the order of a man climbing a ladder. This reading is named after the all-knowing hero and battle-leader, Fionn *(see pages 85–86).*

Select four sticks, ascertaining one at a time which directions give the oracular answer by using the indicator stick. The meaning of each position is shown, right. (NOTE: the indicator stick may give the same cardinal direction to more than one twig!)

4. The realization or manifestation of what you seek.

3. The factor that brings balance to the issue.

2. The unknown factor which influences the issue.

1. The help that is available to you.

SAMPLE READING: Sophie's question to the oracle was about her ongoing recovery from a long period of illness. She drew the following ogam sticks:

1. DUIR IN WEST: The help available to Sophie: *'All seems dark, yet the stars still shine. Trust and endure.'* Having already endured so much, she found this message unwelcome.

2. COLL IN NORTH: The unknown factor that influences everything: *'Be prepared to forgive unreservedly. Do not harbour resentment.'* Sophie's illness had begun after a series of violent incidents in a former relationship. Part of her was still unconsciously engaged in the contracts of that partnership. The coll reading suggested how reconciliation could be achieved. In this instance, it referred not to Sophie getting back together with a man who had treated her badly, but rather seeking peace within herself and letting go of the bad experiences of that time.

3. NIN IN SOUTH: The factor that brings balance: *'Check the co-ordinates. Something doesn't tally.'* The question of Nin asked what was not adding up. Both answer and question puzzled Sophie, but, because this position pointed to how her recovery could be best speeded up, it was obviously important.

4. GORT IN NORTH: The realization of her recovery seemed to hinge upon the oracle of Gort: *'You are being crippled by the envy of others. Defend yourself.'* Sophie mentally considered her friends and acquaintances and could find no rivals or enemies. She was at a loss.

I asked her the question in the oracle of Gort: *'What factors are undermining your abilities?'* Reluctantly, she admitted that she found her mother's continual presence very trying. After her relationship had broken down and she had fallen ill she had returned to the family home. Her mother had welcomed her return but had unconsciously infantilized her while Sophie was weak. Now that Sophie was trying to become independent, her mother's caring presence made her feel like a little girl rather than an adult. This had been a drag on her recovery, she now realized. The oracle had opened her eyes to the situation and allowed her to begin to move on in her life.

I heard from Sophie later that month. A doctor friend, on discussing her treatment, queried whether

her medication was too strong. She returned to her own specialist at the hospital and, after a few tests, her medication level was reduced. She was already feeling much better since the strong drugs had been masking a marked improvement, she now realized. She was now aiming to share a flat with a friend and get a part-time job, so removing herself from the parental home.

Crossed Hazel Reading

This general reading is named after one of the extra or *forfedha* letters, the letter AE or emancoll, which means literally 'twin hazels'. This letter is in the form of two sets of overlapping crosses. You don't need the indicator stick for this casting, since the way you draw the sticks determines the direction of each oracle.

After framing your question, draw two sticks from the bag with each hand and lay them down crossed over each other like a noughts and crosses frame – #. The pair of sticks which lie underneath are vertical, and are read as West and East. The pair of sticks which lies on top are horizontal, and are read as North and South.

SAMPLE READING: James asked whether his plans for an important project could go ahead. He laid Coll and Huath under Saille and Quert as shown overleaf, and read the following:

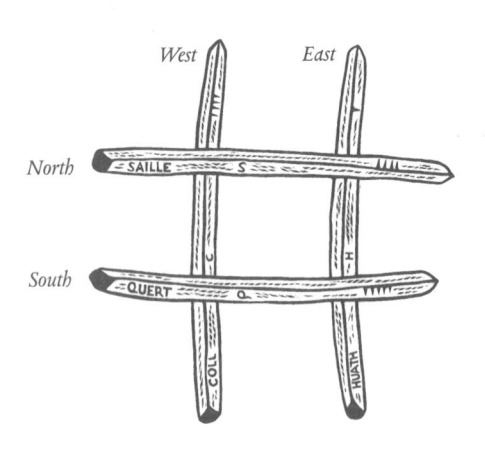

SAILLE IN NORTH: An opportunity has been lost. Keep watchful for the next possibility. What needs to be achieved before the next time?

HUATH IN EAST: Three times you have tried: now the way is clear. How do you envisage your finished project?

QUERT IN SOUTH: Your actions are tuneful and pleasing to others. What is the urging of your heart in this matter?

COLL IN WEST: What is sweet to your taste will prove the most fruitful way to proceed. What is your personal inclination in this matter?

The oracle's advice is that, though an opening has just been missed, things are now lined up for the best possible success, especially if James concentrates on aligning strongly with his own desires. The oracle's

DIVINATORY METHODS

questions pertinently directed him to re-examine the finalization of his project, challenginh him to go back to his own original plans. He had been considering the proposals of an old colleague, but old loyalties might have led him to compromise his goal. By being asked about his own instincts, he was better able to go ahead with his plans.

Branches of the Tree Reading

This reading uses all twenty sticks and can be done once a year to clarify your life and its purpose. As each stick has its own questions about major life issues, your divinatory question is 'show me the shape of my story'. Lay the sticks out like twigs on a branch (*see page 34*). The spread is based on the original sequence of the ogams, but you should randomly select sticks to place in the positions. Roll the indicator stick to find the oracle for each. Note down key words, images or ideas that emerge as you read the oracles. When you've read all twenty sticks, see what overall message you are receiving and read the oracles like a connected story.

This is a big reading. To help you assess what it is saying overall, consider which branches gives you the strongest message. Which gives you messages you need to act upon? If you have laid a twig on its own position, for example the Coll twig upon position nine, the message is speaking with the clearest truth.

CASTING THE WOODS

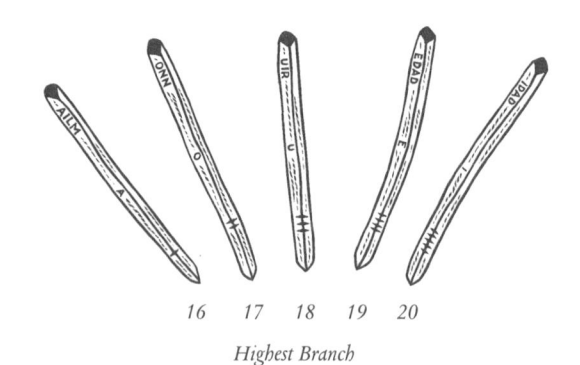

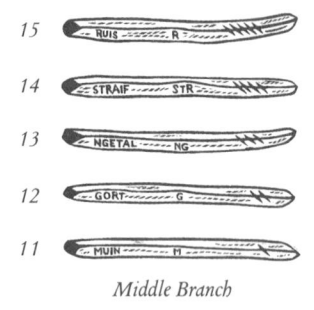

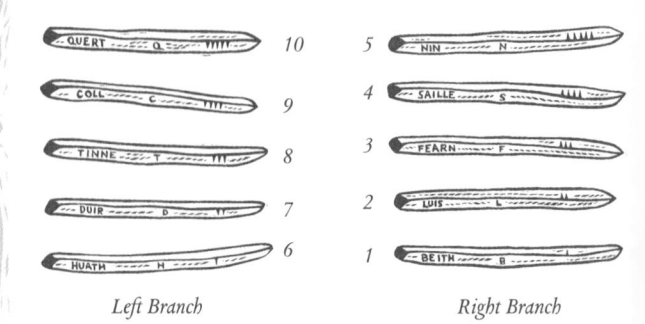

16   17   18   19   20

Highest Branch

15   RUIS — R
14   STRAIF — STR
13   NGETAL — NG
12   GORT — G
11   MUIN — M

Middle Branch

QUERT — Q   10
COLL — C   9
TINNE — T   8
DUIR — D   7
HUATH — H   6

5   NIN — N
4   SAILLE — S
3   FEARN — F
2   LUIS — L
1   BEITH — B

Left Branch   *Right Branch*

34

The Right Branch reveals the roots that are the main source of strength in your life.
1. *My story begins with ...*
2. *The goal I seek is found in ...*
3. *The greatest risk I face is ...*
4. *I find balance in ...*
5. *My clearest life patterns are revealed when ...*

The Left Branch reveals the buds and blossom that represent your personal resources.
6. *My fear and desire are bound up in ...*
7. *My greatest strength lies in ...*
8. *My ability to cope is characterized by ...*
9. *My innate knowledge reveals ...*
10. *My source of inspiration is ...*

The Middle Branch reveals the fruit or progress of your life so far.
11. *The tune of my soul's song leads me to ...*
12. *My skills and aspirations have led me to ...*
13. *Opportunity always awaits me when ...*
14. *I am transformed by means of ...*
15. *I am held back only by ...*

The Highest Branch reveals aspects of your life yet to unfold, the fruits that are still ripening.
16. *My life's achievement is revealed when ...*
17. *My hopes and expectations are met when ...*
18. *My hidden potential is about ...*
19. *Change and liberation is brought about by ...*
20. *Deep memory bids me ...*

Creating your own Readings

Since the ogam sticks are supremely tactile, you may discover other ways of using them as you handle them. Do not be deterred from experimenting and trying new spreads of your own devising. This is especially helpful when you have complex issues that need clearer guidance than one of the spreads above can give. Consider your issue, writing down questions about its many aspects. For example, single-mother Siobhan chose the following questions when considering a move abroad: What effect will it have on me? What effect will it have on the children? What are the advantages of working abroad? What are the drawbacks? What will I gain from going? What will I gain from staying? What scares me most about the move? What excites me? What unknown factors will help me decide? These questions became the basis of a reading, for which she drew nine sticks to gain a better picture.

However complex your dilemma, the ogam oracle can help you bring a greater sense of clarity, as well as suggesting the next step towards a solution.

Interpreting the Oracle

How you interpret the oracle is often a challenge. It is easier to divine for others than for yourself, where it is harder to gain clear perspective. Are we making things up or imagining them? Are we just practising a complex form of wish-fulfilment? Since we live in a society

DIVINATORY METHODS

that trusts the outer senses but suspects the inner ones, few of us are used to believing in our intuitive understanding. Try to suspend disbelief – in the same way as when watching a film or reading a story – so that you are open to the effect of the oracle. At the same time, don't use such extreme analytical scrutiny that you disengage from the message or fail to make the connections it is revealing.

As you gain more experience as a diviner, you will be able to gauge results for yourself, and so feel more confident in interpretation. Learn to gather evidence, notice any subtle or realizations; don't discount this information. Keep a divination journal of the questions you ask and the oracle's answers. Write down the one-line answer from Part Three, or the commentary and any feelings or impressions that accompanied it. Also try to bring together dreams, memories or events that seem to connect with the issue.

Each of us possesses a perfectly good network of information within our own bodies, minds and hearts. Instinct, connective ideas and imagination are what make us subtle human beings: without these three our very survival is threatened.

There is more than one side to reality. The pathways and thresholds which are unseen and unknown to our five senses of sight, sound, taste, touch and smell may be appreciated and understood by our inner senses of insight, resonance, discrimination, empathy and instinct.

Divination and Time

In our everyday world, we live in linear time and space. But the otherworld, whence oracles come, is not subject to time or space. So it is that oracles take place in the present moment. The oracle is out of time and not subject to it. When the diviner consults the oracle, they come to the threshold between the everyday world and the otherworld, where time stands still. The impulse which has kindled our question is part of our experience of linear time. So how do we interpret the oracular answer?

Nothing in human experience is fated or determined. As human beings, we have free will and the choices we make help determine our futures. Often the information given by an oracle can bring us to a clearer understanding of what is staring us in the face, possibly something that we have been ignoring or neglecting. Where we are out of balance with the rest of the universe this is usually the area in which we suffer most difficulty. Indeed, many who consult an oracle complain that it told them what they already knew! However, when we consult the oracle, we are asking for clarification and assistance to make change in our lives. The oracle will not change things for us, but it can help us find ways through and over obstacles and point out areas where action must be taken.

Oracles are the mirrors of truth; they can only reflect what is there under the present conditions of ordinary life. The magical speaking mirror in the story of Snow White irritatingly told the Wicked Queen that 'the fairest of them all' was her stepdaughter; it did not flatter the Queen with lying tales. Neither will this oracle: sometimes it will speak very plainly to you in ways that are uncomfortable. But when we are in possession of the truth, it is up to our human ability to change. When we make honest attempts to rectify disharmony or bring balance back into our lives, then we can consult the oracle again to note the changes. Always deal with your answers in the context of the present moment. The question you ask today will not be the one you ask next month, even if the same issue occupies your thoughts. If you have changed, so will the question.

An important part of the spiritual traditions of the Celtic peoples was the honesty of the spoken word. We are still judged by our intentions, words and actions. This oracle has its roots in the Celtic tradition of truth, honour and integrity. Predictive answers are often expected of oracles and these may sometimes be given. However, this oracle will speak to you honestly and expect something of you in return – the gift of yourself to the life that you live. As it says in the *Auraicept*, 'it is not time that is divided but our own actions'. When we bring integrity and commitment to our lives, we increase the use of our talent and potential, and are more likely to receive the answering opportunities with which the universe responds to our deepest desires and aspirations.

PART THREE

Memory of the Trees: Oracles and Meaning

I can rapidly elucidate every variation of ogam that you ask me about by appropriate questioning.

IN *LEBOR OGAIM* TRANS. CAITLÍN MATTHEWS

This part of the book contains oracles for each of the twenty wisdom sticks designed to be referred to when making a reading. Each divinatory entry consists of the following:

• The Irish letter-name of the Tree Ogam, its equivalent modern letter, and its pronunciation in English
• The tree associated with the letter
• The quatrain or four-line verse which acts as a poetic mnemonic of the ogam letter. These have been composed by the author using the kennings as inspiration and can be used as a metaphorical glyph or picture through which the wisdom of the letter can be seen. These are used fully in Part Four.
• The origins and background to the letter and its kennings. These show the relationship of the alphabetical letter to the under-meanings by which it was remembered by the *filid* poets.

- The treelore associated with the tree – holding an image of the tree in your mind will help connect the letter to the qualities of the tree.
- Four alternative oracular entries of the ogam letter, according to cardinal directions given by the indicator stick. These each have a one-line oracle with commentary, followed by a question. These questions are probably the most potent part of the divinatory process, evoking a strong response and a helpful, honest reaction in the user. Divination is a two-way street, down which both oracle and querent can meet and exchange. If the oracle's answer is not clear to you, try answering the question that the oracle provides in the light of your own query.

Making a reading is an opportunity for you to become interactive with the ogam: relate the oracle's question back to your own original question or starting point. Here, you will become immediately aware of the true nature of the symbiosis between querent, question and oracle. Be aware as you relate the oracle back to your original question what it is conveying to you: this is where your whole array of senses comes into play. Be aware of images, impressions, memories, feelings, sensations or possibly even sounds, connections, smells, instincts and insights. This is the metaphorical and spiritual answer of the oracle, so please pay particular attention to it. Part Four will give you the opportunity to explore this more meaningful interrelation in greater depth.

MEMORY OF THE TREES

Beith B
(pr. be'yeh)
Birch *Betula pendula*

QUATRAIN
First of all hands to clutch the heavenly bole,
The grey-clad youngling seeks high learning's goal.
A cloak of feathers with a bell-hung rod,
He seeks to merit where his elders trod.

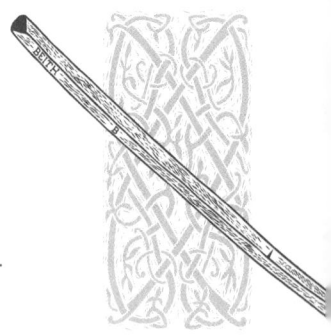

LETTER: Beith is one of the few words of the ogam alphabet that is actually also a name for a tree. 'B' has primacy over all other letters, we are told, because the very first use of ogam was as a warning inscribed upon a wand of birch, sent to Lugh that his wife, was about to be carried off if he did not guard her with birch. The kennings all refer to the birch's appearance: 'withered foot with fine hair, greyest of skin, beauty of the eyebrow'.

TREELORE: Birch was one of the first trees to emerge from the glacial ice when weather conditions improved. Birch twigs are still used in saunas to stimulate the circulation. Until recently, they were also used to physically punish prisoners and the insane as they were believed to expel evil spirits. More historically, they were used as teachers' staffs. Birch twigs can also be bound together to form a besom, or broom. It appears in the Irish law-tracts as a 'peasant tree', meaning that it was commonly available. It is native to Britain and Ireland, growing on light soils, rarely on chalk, and flourishing on scrub and heathland, moors and hills. It is the most easily identified tree, even in winter, due to its silver bark.

ORACLES AND MEANING

B in NORTH
Your innocence shines out clearly.
Do not become a victim.

All new endeavours attract criticism from world-weary bystanders. When such words fall like burning coals into the heart, cast them out swiftly and do not let them smoulder into resentment or worse, so that the lie is believed and your impetus impeded. Returning to the first premise, the innocent person finds justice and peace.

QUESTION: *How would you like to rededicate yourself in this matter?*

B in EAST
You are starting from the very beginning.
Proceed slowly but surely.

Beginnings have their own challenges: the immensity of the plan, the amount of preparation and hard work required and the achievements of those who have travelled this way before can be a heavy burden. It is the qualities of patience and persistence, and the ability to proceed slowly and incrementally, that bring the traveller to that longed-for destination.

QUESTION: *How can this matter be divided into manageable components?*

B in WEST
You wield truth with precision.
Allow love to hone your blade.

Truth is an edged weapon that pares away falsehood and illusion. Whether truth is subjected to plain speaking or to circumlocution, its message drives home. When truth has to be delivered under difficult conditions, it still cannot be compromised. However, it can be offered with the same respect we would wish accorded to ourselves.

QUESTION: *How may truth be tempered with mercy?*

B in SOUTH
The means to sustain a decent living lies within your hands.

Skills and abilities are often obscured by the false divisions of life: career expectations, specialist training and self-limiting goals; these can obscure good gifts. Joy, energy and personal fulfilment must be present in all your work, so that there can be pride in the outcome. Where creative initiative and enthusiasm are kindled, there is the means of life.

QUESTION: *What are your greatest gifts and abilities?*

MEMORY OF THE TREES

Luis L

(pr. Loo'sh)
Rowan *Sorbus aucuparia*

QUATRAIN
The saving herb draws healing through its root,
Dispensing many gifts through every shoot.
Physic of cattle, lustre of the eye,
Answer need's prayer with mercy as we cry.

LETTER: The alphabetical name of Luis does not equate to rowan, which is *caorthann* in Gaelic. Rather, luis is nearer to *lus* or 'herb'. Its kennings are a subtle wordplay on the sound of the word – *lí súla* or 'delight of the eye', as well as references to herbs, 'friend or sustenance of cattle'.

TREELORE: Rowan, also called mountain ash, is popularly credited with being the most magical of trees. 'Rowan tree and red thread' was an old spell used to protect against witchcraft, and sprigs were hung over byre and cradle, for it was believed you could never be too careful where the faeries were concerned. It was also planted in churchyards and outside houses to ward off witches. Rowan wood is traditionally also used for metal divining. It was accorded 'peasant tree' status in Irish law. Native to Britain and Ireland, it grows in woods, scrub and on mountains. It has distinctive red berries in the autumn.

ORACLES AND MEANING

L in NORTH
Allow warmth to flood back into all your dealings. You are freezing up.

Pain sometimes leads to separation and isolation. The tighter pain is held on to, the more unapproachable and isolated we become. When the hurt goes deep, we pass into survival mode and our reactions become automatic, devoid of feeling. Bridge the separation by considering the needs of others – by giving consideration we receive the warmth of affection and respect in return.

QUESTION: *What is the healing that you seek?*

L in EAST
The help you seek lies on a familiar shore. Look closer to home.

Familiarity breeds disrespect and blindness. The solution to the quest often lies near to hand, indeed it may have been in our grasp this long time. Do not despise the ordinary routes. Heroic searches in far-off places may enhance a feeling of self-esteem and effort, but often fail to pay off.

QUESTION: *What or who never lets you down?*

L in WEST
You need to unknot the coil you have made. Retrace your steps and make amends.

When there is a muddle, it is impossible to continue without sorting things out – the coils can circumscribe further action or create further confusion. As with a tangled length of twine, start at one end and trace back patiently to the other end, stopping to untie any knots and snarls. When things are straightened, there can be movement again.

QUESTION: *What needs to be sorted out?*

L in SOUTH
You are steering strongly but double-check the co-ordinates to keep on course.

When a voyage is begun confidently, the mariner is joyful but never complacent, ever keeping an eye on the weather and on the horizon. Overconfidence and boastfulness will not prevent shipwreck, but courage and vigilance will bring the ship safely to harbour. Everything is subject to sudden change.

QUESTION: *What co-ordinates need to be checked again at this time?*

Fearn F

(pr. fyarn)
Alder *Alnus glutinosa*

QUATRAIN
First in the fray, yet modest under shield,
The stripling strikes, causing his foe to yield.
Crimson his skin like bloody gore of silk,
Hiding within the peace-bestowing milk.

LETTER: The name Fearn is derived from the Irish for alder, *fearnóg*. Its kennings indicate the uses to which alder wood was put – 'protection of warriors' and 'protection of the heart' refer to its use in shields, while 'guardian of milk' is a direct reference to milk vessels made of alder because of its water-resistant qualities.

TREELORE: Alder is one of the most sacred primal woods. It appears in the Irish law-tracts as a 'peasant tree'. Its wood is associated with the British divinity Bran the Blessed, who goes down into the Underworld and becomes the oracular mouthpiece of the ancestors. Alder is a water-resistant wood and has been used in the foundations of lake villages for thousands of years. Venice has alder stakes beneath its ancient houses. The bark of the alder can be used as a tanning agent. It is an easy wood to work, traditionally used for clog making. Shields made of alder in use in Ireland during the high Celtic phase have been found. Common throughout Britain and Ireland, it grows on wet soils by rivers, and in woodland and marshy areas. It retains its brown, cone-like fruits even in winter.

ORACLES AND MEANING

F in NORTH
Set aside personal interest and act for the common good.

Acts of sacrifice require that something be set apart and made sacred: this is for the common wealth of all, although it may often painfully spring from personal resources. Sometimes there is more merit in standing aside than in being involved; sometimes personal commitment is required, rather than neglect of duty. Appropriate action now will ensure the outcome is better.

QUESTION: *What is your clear duty in this matter?*

F in EAST
Opportunities lie all about you. Move quickly!

When gifts, blessings and chances abound, there is no need to be modest or retiring. Opportunities freely given are soon seized upon by others standing by. No benefit comes to those who stand idly by, only failure to share in a rare chance. Do not let politeness or a sense of unworthiness restrain you now.

QUESTION: *What chances call out to you now?*

F in WEST
You are hedging your bets. Now is the time to dare and risk.

When it comes to hazarding time, resources and abilities, there are times when natural caution must yield to full commitment, or the risk is just not worth the trouble. If the risk-factor is circumscribed by miserly or selfish concerns, luck has no room to be generous. Counting the full cost makes the result more appreciated.

QUESTION: *Do you dare dance on the edge of risk?*

F in SOUTH
Whatever is beautiful to you is also the truth.

Everyone has a natural sense of order, shapeliness and integrity that spells beauty. This poetry of the soul cannot be twisted or changed without a sense of personal pain or unease. If the seeker follows this sense of beauty to the source, truth will be discovered and the necessary words, actions or silences will result.

QUESTION: *What serves beauty most truthfully in this matter?*

MEMORY OF THE TREES

Saille s
(pr. sal'ye)
Willow *Salix alba*

QUATRAIN
The swarming bees make bright the summer day
With drowsy songs, throwing their cares away.
Kindle a candle when honey flowers appear:
Let blessings quell the stubbornness of fear.

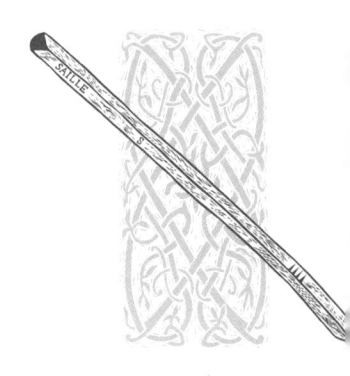

LETTER: Saille is directly related to the Gaelic for willow – *saileach*. Country people in the British Isles still call willows 'sally trees'. The kennings refer to the appearance of the tree itself – 'hue of the lifeless'. They may also relate to the fact that willow, which has male and female varieties of catkins on separate trees, needs the help of pollinators like bees: 'delight of the bees' and 'origin of honey'.

TREELORE: White willow was the wood from which harps were made traditionally, the body being made completely out of one piece. Willow is a 'peasant tree' in Irish law. White Willow is native to Britain and Ireland, but is absent from Shetland. It grows by streams, rivers and in wet woodland, marshes and fens. It is a large tree, not to be confused with the weeping willow which was introduced from China. In Celtic antiquity, its withies were used to make wattle and daub houses, room partitions and many other items. The bark of the willow is still one of the basic ingredients of painkillers such as aspirin.

ORACLES AND MEANING

S in NORTH
*An opportunity has been lost.
Keep watchful for the next possibility.*

The wheel turns round again and again. Impatience often curses the timeliness of opportunity, yet better the plan that aligns perfectly with circumstance than a snatched opportunity wherein all things fail. The observation of life's rhythms and maintained vigilance will help ensure success on the next revolution.

QUESTION: *What needs to be achieved before the next time?*

S in EAST
*It is time to conclude some plans
and to let other things go.*

The availability of time together with the opportunity to finalize a project is often lacking because energies are stretched. In order to reach completion, non-essentials often have to be dropped. Regardless of a sense of things unfinished, now is not a time to complicate matters, but an opportunity to focus on conclusions.

QUESTION: *What essential factors can be finalized?*

S in WEST
*Everything has been washed,
cleaned and cleared. Begin again.*

When things fail or come to nothing due to personal mistakes, a sense of guilt or dishonour may impede future progress and subsequent effort. When there has been misunderstanding with others, it takes courage to broach their company and help again. By releasing yourself and others from old pain, you wash all new.

QUESTION: *Where can you release yourself or others in this matter?*

S in SOUTH
*Your plan is fine-tuned and balanced.
Go ahead.*

The work has been done, all blockages have been removed, there is no necessity to fine-tune any more. Being satisfied with what is shapely and well-balanced is the mark of a good artist or craftsperson. Do not add or subtract anything from your plan. Put your plans into action with the wind behind you.

QUESTION: *What pleases you most about this matter?*

Nin N

(pr. nyin)
Ash *Fraxinus excelsior*

QUATRAIN
No prize in beauty higher than the sky,
Wider than spear can shoot or seer can scry;
The fork that wefts the web can straighter grow
Than any weaving woven here below.

LETTER: The letter Nin has traditionally been associated with ash, which is *fuinseag* in Gaelic, although there is no obvious relation between the two. Strangely, the letter 'O' or Onn, is more directly connected with ash, as the kennings make clear (*see page 74*). As a name, Nin has confounded scholars, who have suggested 'forked weaver's beam' as a possible meaning. There are connotations of 'the fork or rooftree of heaven' – a kenning for the great tree of ancient tradition that stretches from one realm into another. The kennings are obscure and may refer to a word that fell out of usage, 'ending of peace' (perhaps a spear), 'boast of women' and 'contest of beauty'.

TREELORE: Ash is the British god Gwydion's tree in the epic *Cad Goddeu* or 'Battle of the Trees'. Ash's legal status was as 'noble tree' in Ireland, precious for its tall timbers. Native to Britain and Ireland, it frequently grows interspersed with oak in lowland areas. Ash is a very tall tree with distinctive 'ash-keys', which remain on the tree through the winter. Oars, coracle slats, spears and horse-rods were made of ash.

ORACLES AND MEANING

N in NORTH
*Your way is clear.
Obstacles have been removed.*

Whenever severe setbacks have obstructed the path, it is often hard to believe that the journey can begin at last. The path beckons and waits for you – only believe it. Stepping forward confidently, the seeker can sample the experiences of the way with greater zest and enjoyment.

QUESTION: *The influence of what setback is passing from your life?*

N in EAST
*Probe more deeply beneath the surface.
There is more to discover.*

When there has been considerable effort and research, it is easy to be satisfied with the first fruits and findings. However, there may be areas yet unexplored which yield fuller results or reveal wider perspectives. Surface impressions may feel satisfying, but do not be deceived into believing that is all there is to know.

QUESTION: *Are you being too easily satisfied in this matter?*

N in WEST
*You are not harnessing your
full potential. Seek its freedoms.*

After long periods of inactivity or rest, you may feel retiring or unwilling. Sometimes it is easier to rest on your laurels rather than fully engage your potential. When potential is tied up, it begins to be bored and destructive, fuelling resentments and anger. When potential is free to play, the positive effects are experienced by the whole being.

QUESTION: *What is calling your abilities to be engaged?*

N in SOUTH
*Check the co-ordinates.
Something doesn't tally.*

When there is unease that something is amiss but nothing seems wrong, it is time to look at every factor. Do the books need balancing? Discrepancies can creep past the most scrupulous observer when their attention is distracted. The instinct to check up on something is often real, felt in the body, and should not be dismissed as the daydreams of a wandering mind.

QUESTION: *What doesn't add up in this matter?*

MEMORY OF THE TREES

Huath H
(pr. OO'a-huh)
Hawthorn *Crataegus monogyna*

QUATRAIN
Through terror, ancient heroes came again,
Unapprehending of the danger or the pain.
By white blossom, smiling as she stood,
The maiden welcomed them to their soul's good.

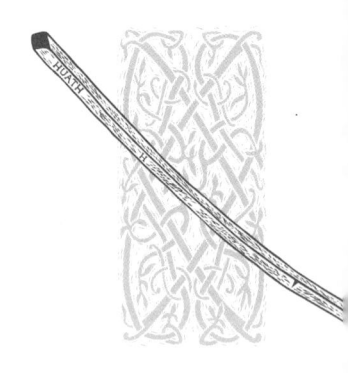

LETTER: 'H' is a letter that is used to prefix words beginning with a vowel. It does not form words beginning in 'H' in the Gaelic language, except loan-words from other languages. *Sceach* is the modern Irish for hawthorn while *h-uath* means 'terror' in older Irish. The kennings for the word are related to fearfulness, 'blanching of faces' and 'difficult at night', and the more obscure 'assembly of hounds'.

TREELORE: Hawthorn is sometimes also called 'may' or 'quickthorn'. It is remembered in the expression 'n'er cast a clout 'til May be out', which does not mean that you have to wait until June to remove your warm clothes, but rather until the weather indicator of may blossom is out. There is great superstition in not bringing may-blossom into a house, for it is considered a faery tree. It is associated with the British giant, Yspadadden Penkawr, the father of Olwen of the White Trefoil in the story of *Culhwch and Olwen*. Hawthorn is a 'peasant tree' in Irish law. Native to Britain and Ireland, it does not grow in northern Scotland. It grows in hedgerows, woods and scrub.

ORACLES AND MEANING

H in NORTH
You are currently too fearful to see clearly.

The loneliness that is experienced when all seems dark is most extreme. But dawn comes, and with it the returning of the light. Colour floods back to the earth and night terrors assume their ordinary, non-threatening forms. When fear gets a grip, even the shapes of day become fearful. Breathe deeply, call upon spiritual powers, rest thoughts upon times when resources were available, allow help to come.

QUESTION: *Who among your acquaintance will give you a clear perspective? Ask for their help.*

H in EAST
Three times you have tried: now the way is clear.

To return to scenes of past failure and attempt to make something work requires much courage and defiance. Such actions are often regarded as foolish in the world's eyes. The determination to succeed is based on qualities which seem to have little worth, but persistence and patience are what clear the way.

QUESTION: *How do you envisage your finished project?*

H in WEST
What seems terrible has another colour. Look again.

The shadow cast ahead by hindsight or backwards by expectation can easily obscure real powers and potentials. Both can create deformities or engulfing fears. Looking beneath the lure of past and future to the present yields another picture.

QUESTION: *What lies beneath the illusion?*

H in SOUTH
Take delight and pleasure in the gifts that are offered.

Unworthiness, ingratitude or low self-esteem are often the excuses to avoid the enjoyment of pleasurable things. When such gifts are refused, a refusal to engage with life can be revealed. Self-preservation is not only about stern survival, but about the welcoming of joy which can transform lives beyond imagining.

QUESTION: *How are you being invited to engage joyfully in this matter?*

Duir D

(pr. doo'er)
Oak *Quercus robur*

QUATRAIN
Keeper of knowledge, master of the wood,
Uphold the tribute for the tribe's great good.
Standing at memory's door with darkened eyes,
Bringing forth fragrant peace that never dies.

LETTER: Duir is directly related to the modern Irish word for oak – *dair*. The kennings of this wood all reflect the high respect in which it is held, 'prized by craftsmen', 'carpenter's work', and the ironic understatement 'highest of bushes'.

TREELORE: Oak is chief of the 'chieftain' trees in Irish law, its timbers being useful for all kinds of carpentry, its bark useful for tannin, and its acorns or oak-mast for feeding pigs. Native to Britain and Ireland, it is usually the dominant tree in woodlands. Its distinctive shape and lobed leaves make it easy to recognize. It is considered to be the greatest of British trees. The word 'duir' may be directly related to the word for druid – an association that is also attested in popular belief.

ORACLES AND MEANING

D in NORTH
Though you feel small, you have the wisdom to outstrip expectation.

A sense of unworthiness or unpreparedness is often felt in the presence of those whose authority and status seem greater than one's own. This may lead to an automatic discounting of your own abilities and resources. However, let your deep instincts and wisdom emerge with confidence and the crown may be won.

QUESTION: *What is your own instinctive judgement on this matter?*

D in EAST
Your abilities have been unused for too long. Use them.

Gifts unused will go sour. There is no virtue in keeping back the impulse of the gift that runs through your being like a river. Waiting for the time of ripeness, it is possible to overlook the signs that the right opportunity has arrived. Do not draw back from the brink of engagement, lest illness or disenchantment set in.

QUESTION: *What is going sour within you from want of use?*

D in WEST
All seems dark, yet the stars still shine. Trust and endure.

No one sees the full overview of life: its entirety is obscured from view. Sometimes even the next step seems impossible because the path turns so frequently, hiding the immediate prospect from view. However overcast it seems at this moment, trust that the stars shine still above the cloud-cover.

QUESTION: *Where are you called upon to trust deeply in this matter?*

D in SOUTH
There is a magic in everything you touch. Now is the time.

Sometimes a strange sense of synchronicity and flow typifies periods in our lives. That time is now. With the confidence and trust of one who knows the intentions of will, soul, heart and instinct, enter into the bequest of memory and enjoy this present moment.

QUESTION: *What is calling you to the perfection of this moment?*

Tinne T

(pr. tyin'uh)
Holly *Ilex aquifolium*

QUATRAIN
Within the burning glead, the dark fire glows,
A whirling brand that threeways, sunwise goes.
Echoed enchantments hammer out the song:
Who spins with this turning shall live well and strong.

LETTER: Tinne, meaning 'bar of iron', has traditionally been associated with holly, although it bears no direct relation to it, being *cuileann* in Irish. The kennings refer to the use of chariots, where holly was used in shafts, 'third of a wheel', or to smith-craft, 'third of a weapon', or to fire or *teine*, 'marrow of charcoal'.

TREELORE: In medieval lore, holly was thought of as a male tree and ivy as a female plant: in medieval carols, the two have a traditional battle for primacy at the time of midwinter. Holly was accorded 'chieftain tree' status in Irish law since it is one of the strongest and most resilient woods for objects that are subjected to stress – like chariot wheel-shafts. Many holly bushes act as boundary trees and are rarely uprooted due to a deeply inculcated respect for them that survives from ancient times. Native to most of Britain and Ireland, holly grows in hedgerows, woodlands and as scrub on hillsides. It is an evergreen and its prickly glossy leaves and red berries make it a favourite garland for midwinter.

T in NORTH
*You are singing the same old song
without regard for the tune.*

Old patterns and slights can warp intention from its true pathway. When old tunes are sung over and over, they can lose their meaning. Friends avoid the singer whose voice has become boringly repetitive. By attuning to the present moment and its needs, by listening to the blessed silence in a place of spaciousness, new tunes quicken in the singer's soul.

QUESTION: *What new song is
waiting in the wings?*

T in EAST
*You have stripped the bark
and see the shape clearly.*

Discernment is achieved by clearly stripping back illusions and perceiving what lies beneath. The five outer senses of sight, sound, taste, smell and touch have five unseen kindred – inner vision, resonance, discrimination, instinct and empathy. By combining these senses as matched pairs, the full picture is quickly understood.

QUESTION: *What truth do your
inner and outer senses reveal?*

T in WEST
The time of sadness is coming to its end.

Unhappiness colours the rich palette of life a uniform grey. Some sadnesses must run their course, especially when they involve grave loss. However, the first signs of a renewed appetite for life will occur in the last phases of the bereavement cycle, like the first green shoots in the iron-clad winter days of early spring.

QUESTION: *What factors
have begun to lift your heart?*

T in SOUTH
*You have planned and practised enough.
Implement your ideas now.*

The wheel has turned full circle back to where it began. Now that a full cycle has been completed, all variations are known. Information once assessed can become memory-resident; the freedom to play with and use it in a practical way has come, now that the shapes and patterns are known.

QUESTION: *What cycle has
been recently fulfilled?*

MEMORY OF THE TREES

Coll c
(pr. Coll)
Hazel *Corylus avellana*

QUATRAIN
Wisdom resides within the secret heart;
Who seeks it fervently will have his part.
Beasts of good sense seek out the sweetest meat,
Men of learning follow craft with even feet.

LETTER: Coll means hazel and all its kennings refer to the tree directly – 'fairest tree', 'friend of nutshells' and 'sweetest tree'.

TREELORE: Hazel staffs or wands have ever been the mark of magicians and druids. Hazel rods are used for divining water, which is not surprising considering how many hazel trees grow over water, particularly sacred wells. Its primacy is recorded in Irish legal tracts, for it is a 'chieftain tree', prized for its sovereign qualities. Native to Britain and Ireland, it grows everywhere except the Shetlands. It grows in woods, where it often forms a scrub layer, and in hedgerows. The hazelnuts of knowledge are dispensed over the healing well of Segais, near the source of the River Boyne, where the salmon of wisdom feeds.

C in NORTH
Be prepared to forgive unreservedly.
Do not harbour resentment.

The offences suffered at the hands of others spring most often from their thoughtlessness or selfishness. Such divisions may arise when all is not clear between us. If honesty and goodwill cannot repair the damage, then it is necessary to discharge the hurt, lest resentment simmer and cause more pain.

QUESTION: *How can reconciliation be achieved?*

C in EAST
Off-load the burdens you are currently carrying.

When too many responsibilities are being borne, the back must eventually break. If overcommitment is causing stress and ill health, lighten the load. If living by impossible standards is causing strain, review the mainstays of your existence afresh. Misuse of personal powers causes them to warp and decline.

QUESTION: *What can be delegated or shared with others?*

C in WEST
What is sweet to your taste will prove the most fruitful way to proceed.

When the tide is flowing strongly towards the sea, it is foolish to swim upstream. Most often our inclinations dictate the most appropriate pathway to take. Those who suspect their own natures of being self-indulgent, falsely denying themselves any allowance, need to inhabit themselves more truthfully and listen less often to the opinions of others.

QUESTION: *What is your personal inclination in this matter?*

C in SOUTH
You are in tune with the universe in a harmonious way.

It is ungrateful to question the joy and wholeness that come as a result of perfect alignment and balance. The simplicity and openness of a child are appropriate when life unreels smoothly. Fulfil your plans with gladness. Do not fall into the complacency of fulfilment, but rather live every day as it unfolds, without any expectation beyond the present.

QUESTION: *What are you most grateful for at this moment?*

Quert Q
(pr. Kyert)
Apple *Malus sylvestris*

QUATRAIN
Dressed in a ragged robe, the idiot goes bare,
Hugging the defunct patrimony of his lair,
While through the boughs a patchwork sun shines free
Where healing orchards beckon over sea.

LETTER: There is no letter 'P' in the ogam alphabet. Because 'P' is a Gaelic invention, ogam has the letter 'Q' – the sound 'kw'. The Brythonic languages like Welsh have no 'kw' sound but substitute a 'P' instead. Quert or *cert* has traditionally been associated with apple, which is *úll* in Gaelic. The kennings are all related to *cert* or rags – 'shelter of a lunatic', 'patrimony of a no one', and 'dregs of clothing'.

TREELORE: In British tradition, the apple is the primal tree of the Otherworld of Avalon or *Emain Abhlach* in Gaelic legend. The orchard is always conceived of as a paradise in Celtic tradition and has none of the overtones of sin and guilt which are attached to the biblical paradise narrative. The blessed apple trees are in the charge of Morgen, the Royal Virgin of Avalon. Her apples are those of healing and restoration. At the foot of Glastonbury Tor the apple orchards still grow today. The apple tree was legally considered a 'chieftain or noble tree' in Ireland, precious for its fruit. The crab apple (*Malus sylvestris*) is the only apple native to Britain and Ireland. Other species have been introduced and interbred. Cider is produced from crushing the fruit and can make either an innocuous or potent brew, depending on the recipe.

ORACLES AND MEANING

Q in NORTH
Stop scratching around in such worn out resources.

When the store cupboard is bare and inspiration runs dry, panic sets in. When a once-abundant source ceases to give water, it is time to look elsewhere. This entails turning away from the familiar, easy pathways to new and unexplored territories. Fresh resources always come to those willing to take this risk.

QUESTION: *What are you still clinging to that is pulling you down?*

Q in EAST
You are acting in a manner unworthy of yourself.

The intoxicated cannot be responsible for their actions, neither can those who are drunk on their own success or ideas. When awareness of self steps beyond the boundaries of good sense, laughter and mockery are triggered in the onlooker. When sobriety or good sense returns, it is time to reset the gauge of humility.

QUESTION: *How is your sense of self-importance impeding you now?*

Q in WEST
There is no advantage one way or the other.

Sometimes when the oracle cannot assist, common sense must play its part. In all decisions, there must be personal responsibility and an equal acceptance of success and failure. Sometimes two pathways lead to the same goal: the advantages of either way cannot be qualitatively assessed except by the walker of that way.

QUESTION: *What action does your generous nature suggest?*

Q in SOUTH
Your actions are tuneful and pleasing to others.

When intentions are attuned to deeds there is a pleasant harmony appreciable to all, although the grace and resonance of such deeds may not always be apparent to the doer. This unconsciousness may be attractive to the unscrupulous, but for the one who follows her heart, the shield of integrity is a protective guardian.

QUESTION: *What is the urging of your heart in this matter?*

MEMORY OF THE TREES

Muin M
(pr. min'ye)
Vine *Vitis vinifera*

QUATRAIN
Path of utterance cleaving the quietened throng,
Each listens to the beauty of your song.
Wide your embrace, affectionately you cling,
While ever on the birds of summer sing.

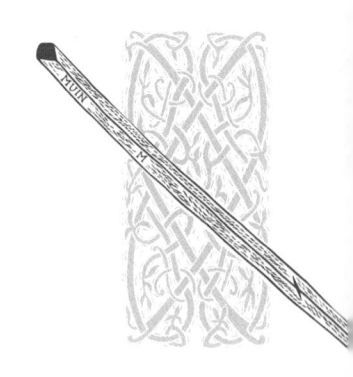

LETTER: Muin is Old Irish for 'neck' or 'back'. The ascription of vine to 'M' is a particularly telling one in that vineyards were introduced into Britain by the Romans, but are indigenous neither to Britain nor Ireland, although wine was imported and traded. The Irish for vine is *finiúin*. The kennings refer to the strength of the back, 'strongest effort', or to the neck, 'pathway of the voice', or to the burden of vengeance, 'bequest of slaughter'.

TREELORE: The vine is native to south-east Europe and is grown throughout the warmer parts of Europe, including southern Britain, where it was introduced by the Romans. Wine was a desirable import to Ireland. The intoxication of its berries is mentioned in the *Voyage of Maelduin*, where the Irish maritime hero, Maelduin, encounters an otherworldly island and squeezes the berries into a cup, so that he falls into a long slumber. On awakening, he orders his men to take the berries and mix them with water to lessen their potent effect, in much the same way as powerfully-fermented wine was mixed with water in the classical period.

M in NORTH
Allow others to carry their own burdens.

By weaving oneself into the lives of others one does them no favours, especially if one's own survival is risked. There are many people whose dependence upon us can leach out our lifeblood. Friendly help is not the same as taking complete responsibility for others. The true nature of a relationship or situation can be unclear if our own needs and desires are suppressed.

QUESTION: *What burdens belonging to others are you carrying?*

M in EAST
Your struggle is not without seeds of victory. Rest now.

Sometimes a conflict cannot be resolved by further fighting. To soldier on without seeking arbitration or resolution through temporary truce is to disrespect the opponent and give them no opportunity to find a peaceful solution. Restoring your energies by rest, you can continue the fight or discussion another day.

QUESTION: *Who is the enemy, who the ally in this matter?*

M in WEST
Bring a lighter touch to the things that matter.

The more earnestly the endeavour is approached, the more life goes out of it. When we play at our work, giving our full energies and intentions to it, our work flowers and is fruitful. To be playful is not to be frivolous – the play of a child is the most seriously intent playfulness on earth. The flight of birds revels in the thermal opportunities of the unmoving earth.

QUESTION: *How can you bring greater playfulness to the situation?*

M in SOUTH
Your envy of another is impeding your way.

The harm that envy can do affects not only its object, but also its source. The potentially murderous capability of envy can petrify the envied as well as clothing the envy in a cloak of obscuring obsession. Motivated by undeclared fears, needs or greed, the envy grows great at the expense of others.

QUESTION: *What is the source and consequence of your envy?*

MEMORY OF THE TREES

Gort G

(pr. gort)
Ivy *Hedera helix*

QUATRAIN
Within the sweet enclosure take your rest,
Unless you come to grapple with the best.
Grateful and giving, steadfast to the end,
To many a poor mouth shall its riches lend.

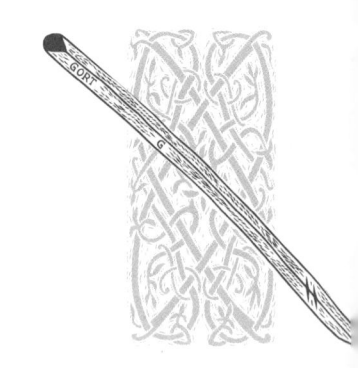

LETTER: Gort means 'field', whereas *eidhneán* is Irish for ivy. All the kennings refer to the field's qualities or function: 'greenest pasture', 'setting for cattle' and 'satisfaction of many'. Since the pasture was the basis of Ireland's dairy production and the cow one of the main units of currency, the grazing potential of the field was important.

TREELORE: 'Ivy for its beauty', says the Welsh text, *Cad Goddeu*. Ivy is not regarded as a tree today, nor does it appear in the Irish tree laws as one. According to several medieval carols, ivy is personified as feminine and emblematic of women, battling forever over the sovereignty of the woods with holly, which is personified as masculine. Ivy carpets woodland and can grow to thirty metres up trees and buildings. It has yellow-green flowers and black berries which are poisonous.

ORACLES AND MEANING

G in NORTH
You are being crippled by the envy of others. Defend yourself.

The restrictions that are placed about us by the envy of others are often subtle and unseen. However, the effect of such envy is all too evident. It is imperative that you do not fall under the spell of the envious or succumb to their messages. Before you are undermined, you must reassert your powers forthrightly.

QUESTION: *What factors are undermining your abilities?*

G in EAST
Whatever is forged in the smithy of your soul will come to light.

The lifetime task of honing the soul is like the work of a blacksmith. It takes continued effort to shape the metal – the application of the creative extremes of fire and water. The soul is a mirror in which all the experiences of life are reflected and refracted.

QUESTION: *What is the source of your soul's truth?*

G in WEST
Your mastery of the currents gives rise to praise.

When deeds and skills evoke admiration, pride and envy are not far behind. Pride in one's abilities should always be tempered by the responsibility for maintenance of the gift. The lightning stroke of envy does not affect one who is so balanced. Mastery makes everything look easy, but it is only maintained by constant practice.

QUESTION: *What responsibility accompanies your gift?*

G in SOUTH
The bloom upon you is borrowed from the misfortune of others.

Delight in another's misfortune is unworthy and shameful, yet the world often applauds the newly jumped-up at the expense of the recently deposed. What we now enjoy can easily vanish away. The theft of another's reputation, skills or attributes adds no lustre to the thief.

QUESTION: *Where or to whom must you give due credit?*

MEMORY OF THE TREES

NGetal NG
(pr. nyayt'l)
Fern *Pteridium aquilinum*

QUATRAIN
Leech out the pain and quell the heavy sigh,
Charms shall bespell the living not to die.
Enfolding is the cloak that wraps you round,
Skill, craft and cunning shall keep you from the mound.

LETTER: Words beginning in 'G' become 'eclipsed' in certain Irish language constructions. This can be seen when *gairdín* (garden) follows an article in the genitive plural – *bláthanna na ngairdín* (the flowers of the garden). Similarly, the Irish for fern or bracken is *raithneach*. The kennings for 'NG' are very obscure – 'sustenance of a healer', 'vesture of a physician' and 'start of slaying' seem all to stem from an older Irish word to do with wounding.

TREELORE: Fern or bracken is called 'destructive fern' in the early Welsh text, *Cad Goddeu*. Once bracken gets a foothold, it spreads quickly over heath and moorland, as well as carpeting the woodland floor. Fern is common to Britain and Ireland, only being absent from exposed locations and wet, limestone soils. It propagates by its spores. We do not regard it as a tree today, but the early Irish termed it a 'herb tree' or shrub.

NG in NORTH
Do not allow the separation to become complete.

Once suspicion, misunderstanding or simple neglect come between ourselves and associates, friends or loved ones, we risk the possibility of wider division or separation. If an outside factor has driven a wedge between you, urgently check its cause and seek to remove it before harmony or love is lost.

QUESTION: *What divides you? What reunites you?*

NG in EAST
Take joy in revealing the dimensions still to be discovered.

Those who delight in quick, easily-won results miss the pleasure in patient discovery. In relationships and in associations, as in creative work, not all is revealed at once: the deeper dimensions and dynamics remain unheard by those who walk away. Patience can be an outer sign of love when it is combined with self-discernment and the willingness to change.

QUESTION: *What requires your compassionate patience now?*

NG in WEST
Be warned. Reconsider before proceeding further.

Survival is based upon observing the often very obvious signs that we each experience. These may be small, beginning as no more than a vague feeling of unease, of something slipping out of place, of something forgotten, but they should be taken seriously before further commitment makes it difficult to withdraw.

QUESTION: *What are the warning signs telling you about this situation?*

NG in SOUTH
Life springs green beneath your fingers. Take courage.

Just as when winter seems coldest, the first green shows itself through the ice, so many endeavours cannot be judged to be wholly lifeless. The dormant green power of new life is about to activate at your touch: this will require your help and encouragement so that growth can be progressive. Do not give up now.

QUESTION: *Where is the promise of new growth in this matter?*

STRaif STR
(pr. straf)
Blackthorn *Prunus spinosa*

QUATRAIN
Reddest of reds, like blood from out the heart,
It lies quiescent in the vat at start,
But rouses to an angry bubbling hiss,
Searing the lip with secret's knowing kiss.

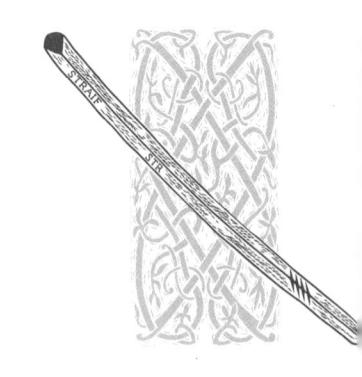

LETTER: ' STR' or 'Z' appears in the ogam alphabet as a letter in its own right. Straif means 'sulphur', whereas blackthorn is *draighean* in Irish. The kennings may all refer to the magical nature of sulphur, which has been seen as central to alchemical processes. These include 'strongest of red dyes', 'increasing of secrets', 'angry heat' and 'seeking clouds'. However, it is also possible that the word is related to *straere*, a wanderer or straggler: a common epithet for blackthorn. The fruits of blackthorn may also be cited here.

TREELORE: Blackthorn is also known as the sloe bush. A band of blackthorn twigs was wound about the tops of fences in ancient Ireland, fulfilling much the same purpose as modern barbed wire. Both animals and intruders were kept either in or out quite effectively by its sharp, thorny branches. Blackthorn was classed as a 'shrub tree' in Irish law. It is common throughout Britain and Ireland, growing in hedgerows, woodland and scrub. It is most noticeable in April when its dark branches are frothy with white blossom. Its purple-dark berries are the potent basis for sloe gin.

STR in NORTH
Separate the grain from its husk before you eat your bread.

Clearer discernment is called for when there are too many mixed messages. The ground of the situation is cross-tracked by inconsistencies. If you proceed without clearly separating one issue from another, the results will be indigestible at a later date and others will blame your lack of preparation and discernment.

QUESTION: *What separate factors need to be distinguished in this matter?*

STR in EAST
Exercise more cunning as you stalk your prey.

When a hunter wants to creep up on an animal he's been tracking, he makes no noise and continually checks the direction of the wind. Whatever your goal, you need to use the same tactics. A little native cunning will be to your advantage. Now is not the time to flag your approach – if you wish to succeed you must learn the art of camouflage.

QUESTION: *What do you need to conceal in order to succeed here?*

STR in WEST
Pour yourself deeply into the song that is singing.

Sometimes a sudden ecstasy catches us up from our place of separation into a state of utter belonging. There is no sense of being divided or different from anything else in the universe, only an exaltation of joyous union. The struggle and difficulties of life dissolve into a peaceful achievement of great surety.

QUESTION: *Where are you being called to union and completion?*

STR in SOUTH
Allow your inner light to shine brightly.

Since the time of full expression grows nearer, you no longer need to conceal your true feelings or abilities. Indeed, to hide your innate self away at this time may prove disastrous. Disclosure of what you are capable of, and of your inner nature, will give the clearest possible signal to those around you who have been waiting.

QUESTION: *What about this matter kindles your deepest nature to fullest expression?*

MEMORY OF THE TREES

Ruis R

(pr. reesh)
Elder *Sambucus nigra*

QUATRAIN
Queen of two gifts, dispensing bounties bright,
Unfolding store of day and claim of night,
Keep strong in honour the undying name,
Hiding from sight the secret of all shame.

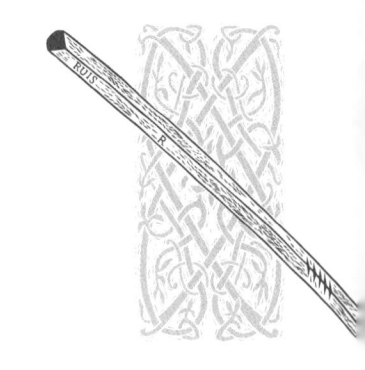

LETTER: Ruis comes from the word 'to redden'. The elder tree is *trom* in Irish. All the kennings connected with this tree are about the blush of shame or anger, including 'redness of face', 'glow of anger' and 'intense blushing'.

TREELORE: The elder is one of the best-known faery trees and, as such, is believed to be unlucky for general use: 'tree that in truth hurts sore'. It is very much a tree of endings and completions. It is classed as a 'shrub tree' in Irish law. Native to Britain and Ireland, it grows everywhere except north Scotland. It flourishes in hedgerows, scrub and open woodland. All the green parts of elder are poisonous but the flowers in springtime and the berries in autumn make both refreshing and invigorating wine. Elder blossom has a pungent, unpleasant smell to it.

R in NORTH
Give bounteously from your store of good things.

The goods, gifts and resources that make you who you are need to be used. If they are kept for some mythical rainy day, their beauty fades, their savour sours. You may possess the very thing that is required at this moment – the lack of this thing or quality may make a great difference to the lives of many.

QUESTION: *In what ways is your innate bounty being called upon?*

R in EAST
Be firm. Balance your generosity with wisdom.

It is easy to be indulgent with those we love or pity, but that is not always what the recipient most needs. Unwise generosity can lead to dangerous dependencies and precedents that may entangle you in unpleasant situations in the future. Dispense appropriate help by all means, but ensure that the boundaries are clearly delineated.

QUESTION: *Where is your generosity outrunning your judgement here?*

R in WEST
Keep a sense of proportion. Some friendly rivalry is to be expected.

Disagreements and bickering between partners and colleagues are seldom serious; though they may appear so to outsiders. Such squabbling is often part of the process by which parity is achieved, especially when respect for the other side is entertained. Humour can be used to keep things on a friendly level, cutting inflated egos down to size.

QUESTION: *What is the funny side of this situation?*

R in SOUTH
Do not let shame keep you from involvement.

Feelings of inadequacy or unworthiness frequently obstruct the flow of life, setting aside the opportunities and chances which you have worked so hard to gain. By concentrating on what only you can bring to a project or association, and by avoiding vain comparisons with others, you can contribute much.

QUESTION: *What perceived inadequacies are holding you back here?*

MEMORY OF THE TREES

Ailm A
(pr. al'yem)
Pine *Pinus sylvestris*

QUATRAIN
What birth-cry calls out first when we take life?
Each echo is the answer to its strife.
The tallest guardian of a windy plain,
Calls loudly to the easing of all pain.

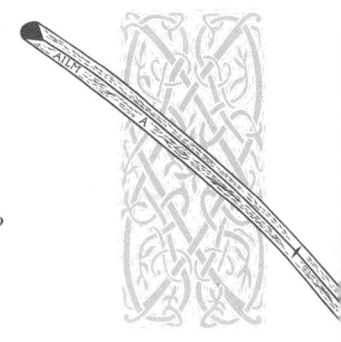

LETTER: The kennings for 'A' are all based upon the sound of the letter, and possibly even the sound of the tree's sighing: 'loudest groan, the beginning of an answer, or the start of a call'. A note in the *Life of St Columba* talks about the two 'A's between which life is lived: the wailing 'A' of the newborn, and the groaning 'A' of the dying. *The Book of Ballymote* offers 'palm-tree' as the associated tree, but the *Auraicept* accepts pine or fir for ailm, although its Gaelic equivalent is *gíuis*.

TREELORE: Pine or Scots pine is accorded place as a 'chieftain tree' in Irish law, for it has some of the straightest timbers. It is native to Scotland and is found across Europe, although it died out in Ireland after about 900 CE. Pine branches were used as temporary bedding, as the ninth century dialogue between the King and hermit shows: 'Oh hermit, why do you not sleep in a bed? Most often you sleep outside on a floor of pine.' It was one of the first trees to grow in northern Britain after the melting of the glaciers of the Ice Age.

ORACLES AND MEANING

A in NORTH
Show the nobility of your nature in your response.

The very best side of human nature comprises truthfulness, strength, love and wisdom. Some directions of this compass of virtues are allowed to waver from their home position, but what stabilizes them is the authority of experience and appropriate response in the present moment. This requires no suggestion from another, but arises spontaneously in response to the situation.

QUESTION: *What is the most ethical response to this situation?*

A in EAST
This matter cannot be judged in terms of black and white.

Within a court of law, cases of guilt and innocence are clearer to judge than those where culpability and truth seem evenly distributed on both sides. In such cases a deeper wisdom is required, taking into account the provocation and loss on either side. Neither side is wholly evil, neither side is wholly good.

QUESTION: *What human compromise can help decide this matter?*

A in WEST
Plough the furrow now if you would enjoy the bread later.

This is a time of hard preparation and work. It cannot be put off to a later day. Avoidance now will impoverish you in the months to come. However, by immersing yourself in the work now, the ground will be made fertile and your work sustain you later. No one else can do this for you, so roll up your sleeves and take pride in your labours.

QUESTION: *What hard work is required of you at this time?*

A in SOUTH
It is a judicious time to hide your intentions from others.

By diverting attention from your true intentions at this time, you gain a breathing space to finalize plans or allow ideas to come to fruition, when they can indeed be revealed freely. Premature revelation can halt the creative process or cause plans to be aborted before they are ready. If your opinions are unformed, remain silent.

QUESTION: *What needs to be finalized before you show your hand?*

MEMORY OF THE TREES

Onn o

(pr. on)
Gorse *Ulex europaeus*

QUATRAIN
Smooth-worn and round, by wind and by sea,
In darkness, the wonder of making grows free.
No joints shown, but joining all hosts to the song,
As wisdom's beguiling makes short cuts of long.

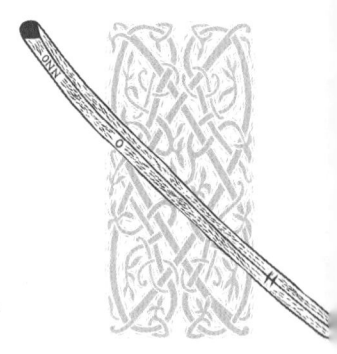

LETTER: The *Auraicept na n'Eces* assigns gorse to this letter in a way that seems contrary to sense, since *onn* is an Old Irish word for 'ash', as well an archaic word for 'stone'. Gorse is *aitenn* in Irish. However, the kennings must be old, since they all relate to ash wood: perhaps the horse-stick is cited in 'helper of horses', while 'smoothest of carpentry' and 'equipment of warriors' refer to ash-wood spears. They may refer equally well to 'stone' or to other meanings.

TREELORE: Gorse is one of the fastest-growing heathland shrubs. The Irish classed it as 'herb tree'. In Irish law, the presence of gorse, or furze as it is popularly called, denotes a place of rough or uncultivable ground. The coconut-smelling flowers of gorse give colour to heathland from the beginning to the end of the growing season. Indeed, it is difficult to find a time when there is not some yellow blaze of gorse blossom colouring the view. After crushing, gorse was once used as fuel, roofing, fencing and animal bedding, as well as for horse fodder.

ORACLES AND MEANING

O in NORTH
Prepare to celebrate.
Your hard work is coming to fruition.

Goals which you have long-planned for seem to take an age to achieve, so their sudden arrival upon the horizon often takes us by surprise. It is time to change gear into completion mode. When everything has been resolved satisfactorily, you will have a chance to honour the time in joyous celebration with those who have waited with you.

QUESTION: *What is coming to completion at this time?*

O in EAST
The cares you have been carrying are about to lift.

When the anxieties and worries of the day-to-day render life dull and featureless, it is easy to become accustomed to little respite and to look forward to no significant change. Before long, the daily grind can become routine. However, now is the time to lift your head and prepare to exchange dogged determination for a more lively attitude.

QUESTION: *What relieving changes do you wish to invite into this situation?*

O in WEST
The shape is not yet clearly recognizable.
Keep trying.

When molten metal comes from the furnace and is poured into a mould, it still needs the smith's hammer to shape it before it can be used. So it is now. What you had thought nearly finished requires more work and patience. Your original plan may require clearer conceptualization. It may even mean returning to the drawing board.

QUESTION: *What still needs to be clarified in this matter?*

O in SOUTH
The way is narrow,
but you may pass through.

Desperate times and situations call for deep reserves of courage and daring. If your resolve is firm, there is an opportunity now to go ahead, but it is not a way for the faint-hearted or hesitant. If you go forward, do so boldly and in full knowledge of what you risk. There is no turning back upon this way.

QUESTION: *Is this enterprise worth the risk?*

MEMORY OF THE TREES

Uir U

(pr. oor)
Heather *Calluna vulgaris*

QUATRAIN
Deep underground there sleeps the summer's brood,
Waking at sun's lance whence the seed was strewed.
Shrouding the dead one, winter turns her face,
Welcoming growth within earth's dark embrace.

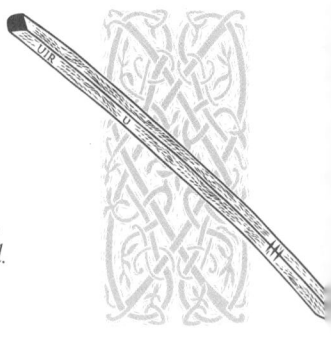

LETTER: Uir simply means 'earth'. The modern Irish for heather is *fraoch*. All the kennings refer to earth or to the growth cycle in some way – 'in cold abodes', 'shroud of the lifeless' and 'offspring of sowing'.

TREELORE: Heather is a 'herb tree' in Irish law. It is abundant on heathland throughout western Europe, growing profusely in acid soil. It produces distinctive bell-like pink and mauve flowers. It was, and still is, frequently used for human bedding by the traveller and hiker, being soft and fragrant. Heather roots do not usually grow wide enough into wood that can be crafted. However, their dried-out gnarled and twisted shapes create curious miniature landscapes. Heather provides a wonderfully colourful covering to heathland and hillside. By late summer and autumn, landscapes take a richer hue from its intense blooms.

U in NORTH
The blessing of the earth lies in the work of your hands.

Whatever your task or work, the skills you possess have the power to reconnect you and others to the deep gifts of the earth. The blessings that flow from your occupation do not only manifest themselves in financial ways, but honour the resources upon which you depend. Tasks undertaken in this spirit of service create reciprocal blessing and mutual support between worker and environment.

QUESTION: *How are you honouring the earth through your life and work?*

U in EAST
Do not deny the spark that flames within you.

Out of consideration for others, or because your personal gifts do not seem to fit in, you may deny your own unique qualities. Just as a flame should not be hidden, but rather give light and heat, so the spark within you – which is the central illumination of your soul – is a radiance that cannot be denied.

QUESTION: *How does your own soul-flame react to this situation?*

U in WEST
It is time to sweep away all that impedes your path.

When there is too much clutter, it is time to spring-clean so that you can see where you are. Sometimes not everything can be saved, not everything still has a use. Peripherals must be abandoned so that the field of focus is clear for operation. By refusing to jettison what no longer works for you, you endanger your progress.

QUESTION: *What stands in the way of this matter?*

U in SOUTH
The love you have given has not been squandered.

Sometimes the efforts that are made to smooth the way for loved ones do not seem to quicken gratitude – this is often remarked upon by parents of their children. However, love that is given here is not without reciprocation. Close companionship may be quietly understated and undemonstrative, but the object of your love does appreciate you.

QUESTION: *How unconditional is your love in this matter?*

MEMORY OF THE TREES

Edad E
(pr. ayda)
Aspen *Populus tremula*

QUATRAIN
Discerning wand that measures every hair,
One stroke of you converts enduring care,
Gives entrance to a long-neglected friend –
To birth's brother and his final end.

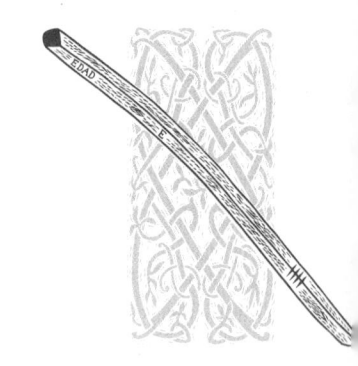

LETTER: Edad is obscure and its only use seems to be to rhyme with the next letter name, Idad. The Irish for aspen is *crithach*. The kenning of 'discerning tree' may relate to the use of the aspen wand as the measuring rod of undertakers, while 'exchange of friends' and 'brother of birch' seem to relate to death.

TREELORE: In Irish tradition, the aspen was feared since it was the measuring rod of undertakers. In Celtic Christian lore it was also identified as the wood of the cross on which Jesus was crucified. Native to Britain and Ireland, aspen grows on poorer soils and in damp, upland areas. It has male and female catkins which grow on separate trees, and so is dependent upon the wind to pollinate. Because its leaves tremble and rustle in the slightest breeze, it is often called the 'trembling tree'. Its soft, pale wood is used today in the production of matches and in paper pulp. Aspen is a 'peasant tree' in the Irish law tracts, being commonly distributed in spinneys and copses.

ORACLES AND MEANING

E in NORTH
You are caught in a net.
Keep calm and consider your strategy.

No amount of struggle and panic will help you escape from this tight place. Only calm consideration will show you your options now. You may have to retreat and go out the way you came in. Some loss of face is involved, but better this than total humiliation. Your own acts have paved the way to this place, but your common sense will save you.

QUESTION: *What is the most expedient line of retreat?*

E in EAST
Strike while the iron is hot – this is your time of power.

This time of action requires the full use of your resources and faculties. It may feel as if you are under pressure, but you relish the chance to be active. Keep relaxed and controlled while you await the coming wave of power that is gathering to a head, so that you can ride it triumphantly to the point of achievement.

QUESTION: *Where is the most powerful impulse in this situation?*

E in WEST
Disentangle yourself and sever relations in order to live.

If your own growth is being impeded, it is better to act forthrightly and separate yourself. Old friendships and arrangements maintained for the benefit of one person only are unhealthy and strangle the other's development. If your attempts to grow are met by sabotage, your very survival is at stake.

QUESTION: *How is your survival called into question here?*

E in SOUTH
Keep faith during this time of disturbance. Love endures.

There is nothing more beautiful than the promise of the heart upheld during a time of trial. What you have committed to perform and honour is the seal upon the contract, your token of love. Rather than seek alliance with justice, you are being asked to show mercy and forbearance. It is a poor promise that melts in the face of trouble.

QUESTION: *Upon what is your promise based?*

MEMORY OF THE TREES

Idad I

(pr. eed'a)
Yew *Taxus baccata*

QUATRAIN
*Hollow of heart, though wisest of the wise,
The hoary ancient gains the poet's prize.
Through countless ages thickening in bark,
Prising deep memory from the forgetting dark.*

LETTER: It has been suggested that the otherwise mysterious letter name, Idad, is paralleled by the Greek name for 'I' – *iota*. The modern Irish word for yew is *iúr*. The kennings refer to the veneration given to this, the oldest of the trees – 'fairest ancient', 'oldest of letters'. To the nature of the yew heartwood, which hollows out as the tree ages, yet still lives, is given the kenning 'sustenance of a leper'.

TREELORE: Yew is the most venerable of trees, often growing to an age exceeding even the oak. In the Irish law tracts, it is accorded primacy as a 'chieftain tree', and carvers of yew wood were particularly honoured above others of their craft. It is native to the British Isles and Ireland, and though frequent in England, Wales and Ireland, is absent from East Anglia, Scotland and central Ireland. It is one of the slowest-growing trees, usually growing wild on chalk and limestone, though it is often found in churchyards, where its associations with death and longevity are living symbols of mortality. It is the prime tree of Ireland, occupying the same place of respect there as the oak does in Britain. Though highly poisonous, yew has been used in the treatment of cancer.

ORACLES AND MEANING

I in NORTH
Cast your nets wider.
What you seek lies in deeper waters.

Your quest is greater than you have realized. Maybe you are searching too close to home? Maybe what you are looking for lies further afield? Looking in all the usual places will not suffice. Be prepared to change how you had envisioned this quest and the pathways will become clearer as you progress.

QUESTION: *What are you truly seeking in this situation?*

I in EAST
The lot falls upon you as the chosen candidate. Take your place.

When we put ourselves forward, we must expect at some point to be chosen. Only the one worthy of the task is fit to accomplish it. You cannot draw back now without loss of face. Those around you recognize your fitness and abilities. Where you lead, others will follow, encouraged by your example.

QUESTION: *What is the role awaiting you?*

I in WEST
Leave the written text.
Memory alone is the anvil.

The knowledge you seek does not lie in any written source. The received wisdom of oral experience is a wiser friend. Gateways of wider knowledge lie within the compass of memory rather than within official sources. This is the land of the soul-traveller who beats out the answer by his walking feet. Step aside the boundaries of time and space to find it.

QUESTION: *What does deep memory tell you about this?*

I in SOUTH
Watch the skies and bide your time.
Your wings are still growing.

While the eaglet awaits its time of flight from the nest, it has the opportunity to observe how its parents fly in different weathers. You are in a similar place of observation where your full potential has yet to be realized, but you can optimize your skills by noticing how they are practised by others.

QUESTION: *How can you foster the potential in this situation?*

PART FOUR

Fionn's Window: Using your Intuition

Our secret name is written by the trees;
Enwrapped within the pithy bark of speech.
Each letter turns the ancient, hidden keys,
The potent syllables beyond tongue's reach;
Words once uttered when the earth was young.
In those vast depths, the lore of trees has root,
Plumbed only when the leaf-green song is sung,
When incantation teases out the shoot.

THE SECRET NAME OF TREES CAITLÍN MATTHEWS

Wherever we find an alphabet, we find magical speculation. For the pre-literate, writing was an initiation into the metaphorical meanings of language, where the thresholds of deep memory are crossed. In the Old Irish *Gospel of St Thomas* we get a glimpse of how the Irish understood the information encoded within the alphabet. In this incident, Zaccharias has taken the child Jesus to school: 'When he had written an alphabet for him he said, 'Say "A". And though the Son of the King did not answer, he knew more.' When Zaccharias struck Jesus for not responding, the boy replied, 'What you have taught everyone, what you have written here for me, the letters that you reckon, I know their sound.' And Jesus recounted his letters for them before their eyes, each letter with its element and its own secret.'

Those secret elements lie within the ogam letters and you have your own unique way into their wisdom through the power of your imagination. In today's world we are taught that imagination only reveals what is imaginary – this is not true. Imagination is a faculty of the soul, in the same way that sight is a faculty of the eyes. In order to discover what it tells us, we have only to step across the threshold of imagination.

The ancient Irish poets who learned 'thrice fifty ogams' and their meanings as part of their oral bardic education, did so by means of association and metaphor. Metaphor is a real, living pathway between our literate and rational understanding and the oral wisdom that is always available to us but often unnoticed. While poetic metaphor runs along the circuits of the brain, it does not yield its best results to strict logic and everyday sense. If you intend to get the most out of the oracle, you will need to relax rational boundaries and allow the metaphors to evoke feeling and memory in you. If you are impervious to the connections the oracle is attempting to convey, then you will simply be unable to receive the answer.

You do not need a dictionary of symbolism in order to look up information, as some people who persist in consulting 'dream-symbols' tabulated and explained in books. Your whole being is a network of symbolic correlation and connection: it draws on your senses, your memories, your background and culture, the experiences you have had in life, your response to nature, animals, people and places. All these provide you with a wonderful array of information which you can use when interpreting the ogam.

Here are a few examples of the way we use our past memories and experiences in every situation. Have you ever caught yourself unconsciously humming a song while preoccupied about something? When you noticed the nature and lyrics of the song, were you surprised or amused? They probably had a great relevance to the topic of your preoccupation in a very immediate way. The part of your brain in which feeling and memory meet supplied you with that song. Have you ever looked upon a scene or object or person and been instantly reconnected with another time in your life? Memory was stimulated and the doors flew open to admit that vanished moment. Have you been reading when a phrase suddenly leapt out at you sparking an idea, an inspiration, possibly a whole series of connections with images or scenes in which you were acting out something of what you were reading? It is in precisely these connective ways that the ogam oracle sticks work and for this reason that you can interpret the readings at a deeper level than that of the written meanings given in Part Three.

USING YOUR INTUITION

Fionn mac Cumhal

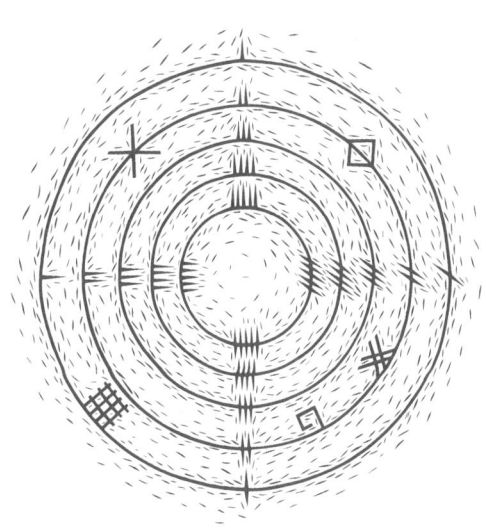

One of the greatest early exponents of the art of memory was Fionn mac Cumhal (Finn mac Cool), whose magical thumb conferred upon him the role of supreme diviner and seer, in addition to his skills as a hero and battle-leader. Fionn was an exponent of ogam and oracular understanding. When faced with a problem, simply by placing his thumb between his teeth, he could enter a trance-like state while uttering a series of visionary impressions. His name is given to an ogam diagram in the *Book of Ballymote*. Fionn's Window, shown below, is composed of five circles which become stem-lines for the four tribes of ogam letters. These are set at the cardinal directions about its wheel: the 'B' tribe in the north, the 'H' tribe in the east, the 'M' tribe in the south and the 'A' tribe in the west, while the *forfedha* or extra letters are set at the cross-quarters. Fionn's Window is an image that can be applied to the mind's eye. It is through the window of inner vision that oracular information presents itself to us in our imagination.

The secret of the ogam letters is much simpler than scholars have speculated: it is not mathematical, nor does it need the linguist's or crossword creator's facility with letters. The unwritten secret of the ancient visionary poets is to use the picture or the metaphorical associations that accompany each letter. In this part of the book, we will explore the deeper uses of ogam to create a personal oracle dependent upon nothing less than our own symbolic frames of reference.

The Ogam Quatrains

Each of the stanzas of the following poem, created from the quatrains which I have composed from the ancient ogam kennings, creates a picture or image in the mind's eye – it is this picture that creates the doorway for a deeper form of divination. The original kennings required an encyclopaedic bardic memory as well as a knowledge of Old Irish. The quatrains have been created so that you can have direct access to the metaphors, image and wisdom underlying each ogam letter in your own language. The Stave of the Wise is the basis for the Door of Memory Oracle that follows. By this method, you can consult the quatrains, and divine answers, without using the oracles in Part Three.

The Stave of the Wise

The wise ones fall and shine, they show and come:
Four seasons, pathways, voices for the dumb.
Converted from the stars to lettered keys,
Opening the door of memory when they please.

B First of all hands to clutch the heavenly bole,
The grey-clad youngling seeks high learning's goal.
A cloak of feathers with a bell-hung rod,
He seeks to merit where his elders trod.

L The saving herb draws healing through its root,
Dispensing many gifts through every shoot.
Physic of cattle, lustre of the eye,
Answer need's prayer with mercy as we cry.

F First in the fray, yet modest under shield,
The stripling strikes, causing his foe to yield.
Crimson his skin like bloody gore of silk,
Hiding within the peace-bestowing milk.

S The swarming bees make bright the summer day
With drowsy songs, throwing their cares away.
Kindle a candle when honey flowers appear:
Let blessings quell the stubbornness of fear.

N No prize in beauty higher than the sky,
Wider than spear can shoot or seer can scry;
The fork that wefts the web can straighter grow
Than any weaving woven here below.

FIONN'S WINDOW

***H** Through terror, ancient heroes came again,*
Unapprehending of the danger or the pain.
By white blossom, smiling as she stood,
The maiden welcomed them to their soul's good.

***D** Keeper of knowledge, master of the wood,*
Uphold the tribute for the tribe's great good.
Standing at memory's door with darkened eyes,
Bringing forth fragrant peace that never dies.

***T** Within the burning glead, the dark fire glows,*
A whirling brand that threeways, sunwise goes.
Echoed enchantments hammer out the song:
Who spins with this turning shall live well and strong.

***C** Wisdom resides within the secret heart;*
Who seeks it fervently will have his part.
Beasts of good sense seek out the sweetest meat,
Men of learning follow craft with even feet.

***Q** Dressed in a ragged robe, the idiot goes bare,*
Hugging the defunct patrimony of his lair,
While through the boughs a patchwork sun shines free
Where healing orchards beckon over sea.

***M** Path of utterance cleaving the quietened throng,*
Each listens to the beauty of your song.
Wide your embrace, affectionately you cling,
While ever on the birds of summer sing.

***G** Within the sweet enclosure take your rest,*
Unless you come to grapple with the best.
Grateful and giving, steadfast to the end,
To many a poor mouth does its riches lend.

***NG** Leech out the pain and quell the heavy sigh,*
Charms shall bespell the living not to die.
Enfolding is the cloak that wraps you round,
Skill, craft and cunning shall keep you from the mound.

USING YOUR INTUITION

STR Reddest of reds, like blood from out the heart,
It lies quiescent in the vat at start,
But rouses to an angry bubbling hiss,
Searing the lip with secret's knowing kiss.

R Queen of two gifts, dispensing bounties bright,
Unfolding store of day and claim of night,
Keep strong in honour the undying name,
Hiding from sight the secret of all shame.

A What birth-cry calls out first when we take life?
Each echo is the answer to its strife.
The tallest guardian of a windy plain,
Calls loudly to the easing of all pain.

O Smooth-worn and round, by wind and by sea,
In darkness, the wonder of making grows free.
No joints shown, but joining all hosts to the song,
As wisdom's beguiling makes short cuts of long.

U Deep underground there sleeps the summer's brood,
Waking at sun's lance whence the seed was strewed.
Shrouding the dead one, winter turns her face,
Welcoming growth within earth's dark embrace.

E Discerning wand that measures every hair,
One stroke of you converts enduring care,
Gives entrance to a long-neglected friend:
To birth's own brother and his final end.

I Hollow of heart, though wisest of the wise,
The hoary ancient gains the poet's prize.
Through countless ages thickening in bark,
Prising deep memory from the forgetting dark.

Within the living past, the future lies,
The future seeded by ancestral eyes.
Between the first and last, a time of strife:
Twixt B and I, the present moment's life.

Door of Memory Oracle Method

Because this is an oral method, it is important that you speak both your question and your impressions aloud. You will find it is important to conceive the intent and frame the wording of your question as exactly as possible. You should give yourself permission to relax, allowing the images or impressions to float up from your imagination without worrying whence they came, or getting hung up about whether you are making them happen. It is the interplay between your question and the quatrain that makes the impressions happen.

1. *Ponder the issue you want to ask about. Frame it as a question. Speak it aloud.*
2. *Draw a stick from the bag to provide the letter of your answer. You do not need the indicator stick.*
3. *Read aloud from the quatrain or verse on pages 87–9 that corresponds to your ogam letter stick.*
4. *Without seeking an immediate answer, without analysing what you experience, allow the images of the verse to work in the melting pot of your imagination. What impressions do you receive from the scene or picture? Enter into this picture or scene. Look about. Be as physically there as possible. What or who else is here in the scene with you? What feelings do you have from being here? Allow the initial picture or scene to open out and develop: it will sometimes do so logically but some-*

times it will change, suggesting further images. Follow them! This is how you track your answer. Sometimes you will engage deeply, sometimes you will witness or experience something unexpected. Those who have poor visualization skills can still draw upon their other senses and impressions.
5. *You may find it helpful to have a tape recorder or mini-disk nearby on which to record your spoken impressions. Or you may prefer to write them down.*
6. *Listen to or read over your findings. Ask your question again, also asking what information your divination has given you. Sometimes the answer is obvious and at other times it is the feeling and emotion of what you experience that give you a sense of where the answer lies. Honour, rather than denigrate, your own findings. The authority of the oracle is responsive to all who honour and include themselves within the web of universal being.*

Since this method is one for which I can provide no key and since every person living will have their own unique experience, I can only give examples of how it might work for you. The querents in the sample readings that follow were each asked to speak their impressions aloud. These were recorded so that they could listen to the divination again. Their own insights are the answer. With a little encouragement and by implementing some of the suggestions and guidance that come from your oracle, you too will find how

FIONN'S WINDOW

trustworthy your own results can be. Further self-questioning of how your question and the oracle interpenetrate will yield illuminating results. Questioning is one of the most ancient forms of learning, directly related to the druidic oral traditions of ogam.

Sample Reading

Moira, an intuitive woman in her sixties, asked *'What is the most important thing to focus on in my retirement?'* She drew Fearn and read the relevant quatrain. She then spoke her impressions aloud: 'I don't like this one at all! but here goes! – I am a man – a young warrior, really frightened – not of the enemy, but of the great long stretch of ground between him and his enemy. It's so wide and he's got to keep running and running forward because it's expected. He doesn't want anyone to see his knees knocking, so he grips his sword tighter and tries to run with style. He gets closer and closer to the other man he's supposed to fight. It's a bit silly really: both himself and the other man are young – they could be friends, not enemies. Beneath all the war paint they're ordinary young men, not warriors. It's like a Mexican stand-off: they wave their swords and snarl but it's like posing, not fighting. I think they're both off to the pub now!'

Moira concluded, 'Of course! It's much easier than I've been making it, isn't it? I can pace myself better and not go at retirement like I did at my job – I've no one to please but myself. I can play by my own rules!'

Sample Reading

James is an outgoing young man. His question was, *'What are my responsibilities in this new relationship with Meg?'* He drew Luis and read aloud the relevant quatrain. He reported, 'I see a plant a bit like the one on the old threepenny piece ... very heraldic. Nothing else.' I urged him to go into the scene and be with that plant. He went on, 'The earth is warm, the soil is crumbly like it's just been dug and sieved finely. I really want to see the rest of this garden. There's a hedge over to my right ahead. It's very dark and tall ... old and protective. It's keeping the wind out of the garden so that the plant can grow. There are cows over to the left: I don't think they should come in here. There's a cowgirl asking to come in. She wants one of the flowers from my plant for her cows.'

Here he frowned and crossed his arms, speaking to the figure in the scene, 'OK, but only one! – She takes the flower head – it's pink – and shakes out the seed into the earth. She's smiling at me. It feels OK. I dig the seed back into the earth.'

Afterwards, we discussed the oracle. I asked him his question and how the scene had given him his answer. 'I tend to get very possessive about my girlfriends. I need to let love grow, give it space and let her come and go. If I do that, there'll be a chance that our relationship will be more fruitful. I think she needs me to be like that hedge as well, to look after her, so that she feels safe.'

The Door of Memory Oracle is both the most advanced and the most simple oracle in this book. It puts the diviner directly in touch with the revelatory and prophetic work of the ancient oral poets who first used ogam. There is a great simplicity in this method because it gives immediate access to the oracle via our own unique associative memory and symbology. But it is also a challenging method because of our contemporary reliance on other sources of knowledge and our distrust of oral learning, inculcated within us by a long tradition of written education. We no longer trust our own realizations as being truthful. Try this method several times, allowing a deeper level of trust and revelation to emerge in your divination.

As you stand at the threshold to deep memory, I would like to leave you with a hidden message left by the author of the *Auraicept na n'Eces*. He writes of the ogam sequence, 'when you speak the first syllable of a two syllable word, the last syllable is future to you: when you have spoken the last syllable, the first is past to you.' However, 'the present time stands for all time.' This riddle's gift is answered by the ogam alphabet itself, where the first letter is Beith and the last is Idad: the Irish word that these first and last letters form is *bí* or 'existence'. Between the past first letter and future last letter of the ogam sequence, we live forever in the present moment of our being.

May the wisdom of your divining forever illuminate the precious present moment of your life!

Further Reading

Dinneen, Patrick, S. *Foclóir Gaedhilge agus Béarla* Dublin, Irish Texts Society, 1927

Graves, Robert *The White Goddess*, London: Faber, 1961

Howlett, David *A Brittonic Curriculum: A British Child's ABC 123*, in 'Cambrian Medieval Celtic Studies' no. 40, 2000

Hyatt, Derek *The Alphabet Stone* Lastingham, York: The Celtic Cross Press, 1997

Jones, Kevin *The Keys of Knowledge: Ogham, Coelbren & Pagan Celtic Religion*, unpublished ms.

Kelly, Fergus *The Old Irish Tree-List*, in 'Celtica' vol. XI, 1976

Leabhar Bhaile an Mhóta (*The Book of Ballymote* c. 1400), Dublin, Royal Irish Academy, ms. source

MacAllister R.A.S. *The Secret Languages of Ireland*, St Helier: Armorica Book Co., 1976

Matthews, Caitlín *The Celtic Spirit*, San Francisco: HarperSanFrancisco, 1998

Matthews, Caitlín *Celtic Wisdom Tarot*, London: HarperCollins, 1999

Matthews, Caitlín & John *Encyclopedia of Celtic Wisdom*, London: Rider, 2001

Matthews, John ed. *The Celtic Seers' Source Book*, London: Cassell, 1999

Matthews, John *The Song of Taliesin*, Chicago: Quest Books, 2001

Matthews, John & Caitlín *Taliesin: Shamanic & Bardic Mysteries of Britain and Ireland*, London: Mandala, 1991

McManus, Damian *Guide to Ogam*, Maynooth: An Sagart, 1991

McManus, Damian *Irish Letter-Names and their Kennings*, in 'Eriu', vol. XXXIX, 1988

Meroney, Howard *Early Irish Letter-Names* in 'Speculum', vol. XXIV, 1955

Minahane, John *The Christian Druids* Dublin: Sanas Press, 1993

O'Boyle, Seán *Ogam: the Poets' Secret*, Dublin: Gilbert Dalton, 1980

O'Cuív, Brian *Irish Words for 'Alphabet'*, in 'Eriu' vol. XXXI, 1987

Sanas Cormaic ed. Kuno Meyer, Felinfach, Llanerch Publishers, 1994 (in Irish)

Acknowledgements

Thanks to David Hyatt for kind permission to quote from his book. I am very grateful to Jane Gubb for having carved the prototypes from which these ogam sticks are made. Love and thanks to John for giving me space to develop this oracle from our shared obsession with ogam. Thanks also to the vision and support of Ian Jackson, Nicola Hodgson and all the team at Eddison Sadd who are always such a professional treat to work with.

The Author

Caitlín Matthews is an exponent of the living spiritual practice of the Celtic and ancestral traditions of Britain. She is the author of many books including *The Encyclopedia of Celtic Wisdom* and has been responsible for divinatory systems such as *Celtic Book of the Dead* and *Celtic Wisdom Tarot*. Her work has been inspirational to thousands of students who have crossed their own thresholds to find spiritual wisdom. She has a shamanic practice in Oxford. With John Matthews and Felicity Wombwell, Caitlín is co-founder of the Foundation for Inspirational and Oracular Studies which teaches shamanism and encourages respect for the sacred arts and traditional oral lore. Visit their website on *www.hallowquest.org.uk* or send £8 (within UK) payable to Graal Publications or send US $25 bills (no non-sterling cheques please) for four issues of Hallowquest Newsletter to Caitlín Matthews, BCM Hallowquest, London WC1N 3XX, UK.

Eddison•Sadd Editions

Editorial Director: Ian Jackson
Editor: Nicola Hodgson
Proofreader: Michele Turney
Art Director: Elaine Partington
Project Designer: Brazzle Atkins
Production: Karyn Claridge, Charles James